GHOST TOWN
TREASURES

GHOST TOWN TREASURES

BY LAMBERT FLORIN

CONTENTION CITY was named for large Contention Mill, named, in turn for Contention Mine in neighboring Tombstone, Arizona. Legal title to rich mine was settled only after extensive litigation. Site of town, selected because of available water to operate mill, is on east bank of San Pedro River. First street laid out along stream was called Front, then came Main and San Pedro. When railroad was built to Contention City it also followed river. Genial guide of Bird Cage Theater in Tombstone, William Hunley, identifies lonely ruins pictured here as once busy railway depot.

SUPERIOR PUBLISHING COMPANY-SEATTLE

FIRST EDITION

Printed in the United States of America

By the Dunham Printing Company

*GHOST TOWN TREASURES is
dedicated to David C. Mason, M.D., whose
assistance has made the series possible.*

FOREWORD

The search for old, historic towns, some dead and forgotten, some with a spark of life and some still lively, has a certain urgency. Those in the first category, the long abandoned places, are fast fading away. Time, aided and abetted by man's vandalism, take its inexorable toll. The scene in any given ghost town changes from year to year as buildings collapse or burn or are deliberately torn or razed— this last most likely to happen in towns still partially occupied or ones revived due to some newly established industry. In these the old relics are often removed because their value is underestimated or they are considered incompatible with progress.

A few examples of these so changed, accidental and deliberate, will illustrate what is happening. Last summer a trailer was parked near a picturesque little group of old buildings standing for many years as the main attraction in the old cow town of Antelope, Oregon. A fire started in the trailer and spread to the dry-as-tinder saloon, and in moments the entire cluster including the barber shop filled with relics of a bygone day was in ashes.

At New Era, Oregon, one survivor of the old town was a small, false-fronted building that had been a Wells Fargo Station and pioneer post office-store. Last autumn this little gem was torn down. It stood beside the highway on the route south from Oregon City and was considered an "eyesore".

In the Anaconda, Montana, area is the site of an old mining camp, once a picturesque town called Black Pine. When Muriel Sibell Wolle visited the camp she made several charming sketches of the buildings, later using them in her definitive book, MONTANA PAY DIRT. When this reporter arrived at the place after a long, grinding trip up the rocky grade he found the town razed. Not a structure remained. A new mining company had started operations there, found the "shacks" in the way and leveled them with a bulldozer, completing the destruction by setting fire to the ruins.

Some mining camps were constructed largely or entirely of sun-dried brick or adobe, such as Ballarat at the edge of the Panamints in California's desert country. Rain in such areas is normally a rarity but does sometimes descend with a vengeance and will dissolve whole buildings especially the roofless ones.

When Dr. David Mason and I, on a joint vacation trip several years ago, first visited Bodie, California, we were fascinated but shocked to see how much of the once-extensive town had disappeared, mostly by the ravages of several fires. As avid amateur photographers we went to work immediately, recording as many buildings and scenes as we could during the rest of that day and much of the next when the light changed.

Bodie came at the end of a mountain climbing and botanizing trip in the High Sierra and was the beginning of a systematic search for other old camps which we could preserve on film. From that start came this series of books picturing so much of so many ghosts and near ghosts, and relating some of their histories. David's yearly vacation is limited to two weeks, after which he must return to duties at hospital and office, this reporter continuing the quest for the entire summer or a longer period and ranging from the Arctic Circle to Mexico. The following winter is filled with film developing, enlarging the prints and recording the stories of places visited as well as planning trips to new places the following season.

Ghost town hunting as a hobby attracts more people every year. Just searching out the forsaken camps is absorbing enough but the hunter will find many side interests. Among them perhaps will be photography for he will want to keep a picture record of the conquests. For some a 35mm camera lifted to the eye, exposing a color slide will suffice. It is a quick operation and the color will please. More difficult and possibly more satisfying is making good quality negatives in black and white. Carrying home several rolls of film, the vacationist can extend his summer's pleasures into long winter nights. The high point comes with the projection of his negative on the enlarging easel. For here is creation, the making of something unique, by selecting a portion of the entire scene most pleasingly composed. In making the exposure thin areas in the negative can be held back, dense ones encouraged by longer exposure. As the image becomes visible in the developing tray there is always an element of suspense and the hope for a masterpiece.

The production of a top quality print which would merit a frame, requires a good negative. As with all other photographic processes, plenty of literature is available on the subject, but we consider a few factors essential. First, the tripod. This slows the picture taking but permits more careful composition and allows longer exposures with smaller apertures used, which results in sharper detail over a deeper "depth of field." A good exposure meter helps in obtaining a properly exposed image. Light filters make the difference between an ordinary negative and a striking one, even though both might be otherwise carefully exposed.

This sort of pleasure is so different from the more superficial exposing of slides, leaving the finishing to others, that most camera clubs now find themselves divided, with meetings for the slide takers and those for the print makers. This particular ghost town hunter takes color slides for lecturing to large groups, the black and white studies for our books.

But photography isn't the only bonus. An ever-changing terrain produces a variety of plant life, trees and flowers. The most insensitive person would be impressed by the snowy, fragrant display of a full-blooming bush of "mock orange," the Syringa or more properly, *Philadelphus* (state flower of Idaho), or the crowning glory of a mass of satiny blossoms topping an otherwise repelling cactus. Trees will vary from the dwarfed spruces of the sub-arctic tundra to lush oleanders running wild in some abandoned Arizona mining camp, strangely independent of any water supply.

Equally evident will be the changing aspects of bird and animal life. The writer was astonished at his first view of a flock of blackbirds in a marsh near Genoa, Nevada — not plain, black blackbirds but birds with brilliant yellow heads! Golden eagles soaring over the Blue Mountains in Oregon are a thrilling sight. Anyone whose contacts with coyotes has been limited to the pitiful, mangy specimens in roadside "zoos," will be amazed at the beauty of the animal loping through the sagebrush in its natural habitat.

It is a rewarding fact that our popular books of ghost and near ghost towns have brought many hitherto unknown spots to public attention and attracted many visitors. We join with Muriel Sibell Wolle, Nell Murbarger and others in constantly reiterated pleas to scout out the towns for personal pleasure and help prevent vandalism.

We like to think none of our readers would carry off souvenirs such as bricks from some crumbling structure or bleached wooden headboards from an old grave. In support of the hope are many letters such as one from 17-year-old Don Cameron of Grandview, Missouri, who wrote: "Aren't you afraid of the responsibility in exposing some of these old towns to so much publicity?" Obviously Don and other readers of such integrity can be trusted to take away nothing but pictures and leave nothing but tracks.

On the subject of headboards, the old burial grounds are as full of history and interest as the towns themselves. Many of the original wooden headboards, usually dated before the turn of the century, are nearly or entirely illegible due to weathering. In photographing them, a strong side-light (as in the Powell Landusky marker pictured in this volume) will often bring out the still slightly raised lettering, making it partially readable. This

MODERN MILWAUKIE OREGON, is far from ghostly but treasures historic Pioneer Cemetery. Burying ground is full of early day markers, many connected with events and stories of Butteville, Champoeg and neighboring towns detailed in this book. The **Lot Whitcomb** was first steam-powered craft built on the Willamette River, constructed in 1850, and fitted with machinery from San Francisco. Built by Lot Whitcomb with money raised through sale of stock to pioneer residents, it was launched at 3 P.M. Sunday afternoon, Christmas Day of 1850. In helping celebrate launching, Capt. Frederick Morse of Schooner **Merchantman,** set off small, seldom used cannon from his ship. Rusty weapon exploded, iron fragment hitting Capt. Morse in neck, nearly decapitating him. He died instantly. Despite tragedy, festivities continued three days. Stone marker stood unviolated for nearly 100 years, was then found broken, car tracks indicating vandal had deliberately run over it.

photographer has spent many hours waiting for the sun to get around to just the right position to properly illuminate an old headboard. And many memorials to loved ones resulted in spectacular or quaint monuments. There was incentive to create something novel or beautiful, sometimes resulting in a weird effect.

Seldom were facilities available locally for the sculpturing and carving of elaborate stones. "Copy" of names, dates and sentiments were hand-written and sent to some large center such as Salt Lake City or San Francisco. Sometimes when the finished marker arrived it would display ludicrous errors. But by that time the first emotional surge was gone and the stone would usually be erected anyway.

There was the time Bodie, California, wished to honor its first citizen, William Bodey (his own spelling). The townspeople imported a sculptor to chisel out a suitable monument to the long neglected founder of the town, using a chunk of native granite. Bodey's bones were dug up from his lonely grave and reinterred in the cemetery. The stone artist arrived and went to work. He finished the ornamental urn at the summit of the imposing shaft and was ready to inscribe the name of Bodey on the side. Then came news that President James A. Garfield had been slain by Charles J. Guiteau. Public emotion over the assassination so overshadowed homage to William Bodey that a committee ordered the sculptor to change the inscription to: "TO THE MEMORY OF JAMES A. GARFIELD." The orders were duly carried out and the monument was erected in the cemetery with a ceremony — but Bodey's new grave remained unmarked, few today knowing its location.

The photography and necessary research for the production of the Ghost Town Series has uncovered so much material and so many interesting pictures of the old cemeteries and markers that a photo-history is in progress, tentatively titled *Boot Hill Revisited*.

The schematic maps at the head of each group of towns in this book are, as we have stated before, to be used in conjunction with the latest highway maps. These may not indicate the old town but do include more detail and the most recent highway numbers. It cannot be too strongly stressed that the searcher should make local inquiry if the road seems questionable as dirt roads can deteriorate in a few days in heavy rains, fast melting snow or new snow at high altitudes. It is always a good idea to carry a spare can of gasoline as filling stations are often far apart. Good hunting!

The end paper design and other drawings in Ghost Town Treasures, as in other volumes of the series are done with water color and charcoal technique. They are the work of artist-doctor David C. Mason, M.D., of Beaverton, Oregon.

TABLE OF CONTENTS

CALIFORNIA

Tropico 11
Gold Camp 11
Randsburg 21
Johannesburg 21
Garlock 22

WASHINGTON

Frankfort 27
Knappton 31
Deep River 33
McGowan 34
Altoona 35
Vader 37
Olequa 39
Maryhill 73

OREGON

Mayger 69
Wauna 41
Apiary 45
Natal 47
New Era 52
Butteville 55
Champoeg 59
Buena Vista 65
Ortley 69

MONTANA

Sandusky 67
Ruby Gulch 83
Zortman 87

IDAHO

Warren 89
Mount Idaho 95

COLORADO

Pitkin 97
White Pine 102
Ohio City 107

NEVADA

Paradise Valley 109

UTAH

Sego 113

NEW MEXICO

Folsom 121
Watrous 126
Cimarron 130
Dawson 136
Koehler 140
Colfax 146

ARIZONA

Ehrenberg 148
Tyson Wells 154
Quartzsite 155
Salome 157
Vulture City 160
Contention City 167
Fairbank 170
Charleston 173

BRITISH COLUMBIA

Sandon 177

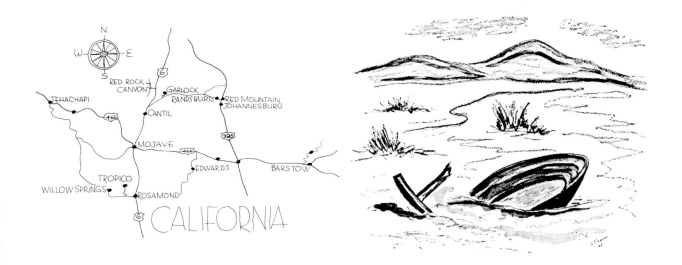

GOLD CAMP AND TROPICO MINE, CALIF.

Potter's clay, that humble substance used to make the feet of idols and sewer pipe, had a special meaning for Ezra Hamilton. It not only solved a problem for his Los Angeles Pottery Co. but led to lush living for himself, his goldfish and silkworms.

The need for drain tile in the Los Angeles area was acute around 1878 when booming expansion was eliminating the privy and bringing the plumbing inside, The pottery concern was able to make the tile but it needed better quality clay than the local soil produced. So Ezra Hamilton jumped at the chance to buy a carload of fine clay from the sample submitted by Dr. L. A. Crandall.

This clay was red, conspicuous in the formations of sandstone, volcanic tuffs, dacite and rhyolite in the hills bordering the north side of Antelope Valley, about five miles from the town of Rosamond, which was some fifty miles from Los Angeles. Dr. Crandall had been looking for gold here and thought the clay might have some value.

It did and was soon being dug out of Crandall's hill in huge quantities and shipped to the Los Angeles tile plant. Hamilton balked at the large shipping costs and in 1882 bought the property from the doctor, at the same time taking out two additional mineral claims, labeling these Pottery 2 and 3.

As Los Angeles boomed so did the tile works but in the early '90s both slowed down. Enterprising Ezra took to panning out some of the clay in his desert hill and found some bright yellow particles that turned out to be gold.

Now more excited than he was over the original clay sample, he and his son Truman set out for

Rosamond as a team. At the clay pits they searched diligently on the north side of the hill, washing pan after pan, always finding a few specs of gold. Then in a gully they found several nuggets and then came a pan in which almost all the dregs were pure gold. Ezra said later: "I looked at that gold. It was rough and lay among broken stones, not gravel. I says to myself, it's a native of this place." In 1896, after more searching for the lead from which the float came, he located it in one of the most exposed spots near the ridge of the hill. An assay showed samples around $35 per ton.

Hamilton returned to Los Angeles, quietly closed out his interests, and returning to the Joshua trees in the desert, set about staking claims. Father and son became acquainted with a colored man who had a ranch south of the hill, one Charles Graves. They became close friends and Graves accepted Hamilton's invitation to stake out any claim he might fancy on the eastern quarter of the hill. "We've got plenty," Ezra said, "and we think you would make a good neighbor." Graves, who had left his Kentucky home in 1882, staked out two claims of the usual size near his ranch, 600 by 1500 feet, naming them Home No. 1 and Home No. 2.

With two other sons, Lester and Fred, joining Truman, Ezra Hamilton devoted his entire energies to the prospective mine. The first ore removed from the hard outcropping was that which showed the good assay at the start and the first payment check was for $4,600, spent for further ore removal and a little two-stamp mill, erected at what would be the Lida tunnel. It was powered by a small steam engine and to fire it the surrounding desert was

stripped of sagebrush, Joshua trees and ocotillo stems, the fuel flaring up and dying down like paper. When it was gone the Hamiltons had to import solid wood from the Sierra, hauling it across the Mojave Desert by wagon.

In two years it was clear they had more claims than they could work so they sold one for $100,000. After the Los Angeles TIMES printed a feature story on the big sale, Dec. 12, 1900, prospectors, promoters and legitimate investors flocked to the scene to make hay while Hamilton's sun shone. And instead of the Hamilton's vein pinching out at a shallow depth, it improved as the mine deepened. They bought the old stage station site at Willow Springs where there was a generous supply of water and erected a new five-stamp mill there.

The fame of the Hamilton mine reached St. Louis, for the World Exposition there asked Ezra Hamilton for an exhibit and he sent one to make all eyes pop. Some of the ore specimens had solid gold sticking out of the quartz matrix and would assay at about $90,000 to the ton. The three Hamilton boys went to the fair on funds derived from a ton of ore each from the stope of the Lida — $5,000 for each son.

Hamilton now had time and money to carry out some of the plans for Willow Springs, the first a health resort for those suffering from lung trouble. To the buildings he added a large goldfish pond with landscaping — an oasis contrasting markedly with the uncompromising desert. And the grapevines did so well additional plantings were made to support a small winery. Also planted were mulberry trees, the leaves of which would feed his hungry silkworms.

The next few years saw many changes on the hill. Charles Graves leased his claims to the Hoyt Brothers Company and they in turn sold all rights to the Big Three Mining and Milling Co. which combine then bought several of Hamilton's claims. A J. B. Freeman was president of a firm that "perfected" a new dry wash system which would have saved hard-to-get water had it been more successful. The mill, erected in 1904 to extract gold from the Big Three holdings, operated at a loss for several years and at length the discouraged mine owners allowed the mine workings to stagnate. By this time Hamilton had sold the rest of his holding and things on the hill were very quiet.

In 1907 the mine complex received a temporary shot in the arm, mainly in the form of promotion by J. M. Overshier, president of the Tiger Head Min-

SIMULATED MINING CAMP CEMETERY, another exhibit at Gold Camp, typical of many found in desert mountains around Tropico.

EZRA HAMILTON makes spectacular discovery of gold on crest of Tropico Hill in 1896. (Photo courtesy Goldcamp Museum, Burton's Tropico Mine Tours).

ing Co. He made some pretense of opening the mines while active with stock selling, then quietly decamped.

After the Antelope Mining Co. took a one year lease in 1909 with no results, another company took over. Some of the stockholders came from a small community called Tropico, near the present Forest Lawn Memorial Park at Glendale, and they named their group the Tropico Mining and Milling Co. President V. V. Cochrane, with leading stockholders B. Gross and O. S. Richardson, were successful in consolidating the many past ownerships and in having them patented. The Tropico Company was successful also in finding paying values and operating the mines until 1934 with a one year break in 1923. A J. F. White held the lease for that period.

When the Antelope Valley was being opened up by real estate promotions in 1900, one flamboyant advertisement in FIELD AND STREAM lured at least one family, the Burtons with four sons, one twelve-year-old Clifford. The family settled on a ranch in the valley not far from the present Mira Loma, now site of the county prison.

Young Clifford worked on the ranch with the others but at eighteen took off for the rocky desert hills with a friend, Mel Sanford. The two made a good strike near Ballarat in the Death Valley area and sold it for $4,500 to a well known mining figure, "January" Jones. Clifford used his share to study geology, mining techniques and refining methods, attended a mining and assay school in Los Angeles, returning to Antelope Valley and a job at the Tropico mine in 1912.

Burton was able to suggest methods to improve milling that eliminated many of the worst difficulties and in 1914, as mine superintendent, he sent for his favorite brother Cecil. The Tropico then humped in production, operating profitably until 1917 when the war forced a near closure.

Returning from the service in 1920, the Burton brothers again went to work for Tropico but rising costs and decreasing ore values made the going hard. Many stockholders sold out to the Burtons who eventually had a controlling interest. In the early '30s a number of farmers turned miners began finding small amounts of good ore in the hills and trucked it to the Burton mill for "custom" refining. Then came President Roosevelt's edict raising the price of gold from the prevailing price of $20.07 per ounce to $35. The Burton Tropico mine was on the way to another bonanza.

Clifford Burton was able to see the best gold values would increase in a westerly direction and accordingly stopped all other extensions, opening up new tunnels from several lower levels, proving there was more gold here than even during Ezra Hamilton's heyday. More and more mines in the hills, as far away as Death Valley and Twentynine Palms, were sending in custom jobs until the Burtons were forced to expand their mill facilities to handle ore from four hundred mines.

They also established a "trading post" on the Tropico premises, outfitting and grubstaking prospectors, selling equipment and supplies to established miners. The Tropico mine in 1942 was extending its operations to the Ruth mine near Trona, California, and the Fortuna near Yuma, Arizona,

LITTLE FIRE HOUSE is featured at Gold Camp. Fire was main enemy of most mining camps, particularly in parched desert areas and Volunteer Fire Department was important social factor. Members often put on shows, contests in speedy trips to fires, unreeling of hose from carts. Unfortunately, when actual alarm sounded, fire laddies were often relaxing in town bistros and might forget which end of hose was which.

15

HILLS AND GULCHES around Tropico mine are included in "Rosamond formation", offer everything from clay to gold. Here on northeast slope of what would be called Tropico Hill, Dr. L. A. Crandall found samples of good quality clay. Discovery of material and timely acceptance by Ezra Hamilton for his Los Angeles pottery works diverted further prospecting for gold until after business recession slowed tile production. Hamilton gophered entire hill, evidence shown here in small dumps scattered over hill. Large excavation in foreground shows enormous amounts of clay were removed and shipped to Los Angeles.

when the whole operation ground to a halt with the government curtailing gold production with order L.208.

Keeping the mines in shape through the second World War was a hard struggle but the glad day did come when the Tropico was allowed to reopen. But now costs had risen to new peaks, machinery had deteriorated, some needing expensive replacement. Miners' wages had risen to a level never before heard of and everything was inflated except the value of the end product, gold being frozen at the price that had seemed so high in pre-war days—$35.

Cecil Burton died in 1947 and Clifford attempted to carry on but was felled by a fatal heart attack two years later. His son, Clifford G. took over, making a gallant struggle to regain the Tropico's former glories but the case was hopeless and in 1956 the Tropico closed down again. This time the pumps were withdrawn and the water level started to rise. Probabilities indicate it will eventually reach to between the 300 and 400 foot levels, flooding all workings below that depth.

The property stood idle until January 1958

when a group composed of Mr. and Mrs. Glen A. Settle, Mr. and Mrs. George F. McNamee and Eric Burton obtained a lease from the Burton Company with the intention of preserving the mine property, keeping it intact and establishing a museum site to bring back the glamorous aspects of early gold mining days. Earlier Glen Settle married Dorene, daughter of Clifford G. Burton, and became assistant manager. The couple has furnished much material for this story of Tropico and the group has moved in many old structures from almost inaccessible old mining camps in nearby desert and mountains. Included are a mine boarding house, railroad section house, freight depot, post office, mine superintendent's home and first school house built in Palmdale. They are grouped along a "Main Street" to create the illusion of a genuine mining camp.

The Tropico Gold Camp is closed to visitors in summer due to extreme desert heat but there are weekend mine tours the year around as the underground levels are always cool. The old mine is intact, almost ready for reactivation should gold values rise to practical levels.

GOLD CAMP is on-site museum of mining and area history. Buildings in old town are authentic, some salvaged from destruction in Palmdale, Rosamond, etc., others from more remote camps where protection from vandals and fire is impossible. Famous Tropico mine is shown in background, dumps and buildings on hillside. Mine is practically intact after days of inclosure in 1956.

RANDSBURG, CALIFORNIA

Frederick Mooers was a newspaper man but he would never have been able to put the fire and excitement into a paragraph that he did in his eyes when he saw the particles of gold. "Boys!" he yelled to his two partners. "We've struck it! There's no need to look any farther."

This was the gold that started the Rand mine, that gave the name Rand to the mountains and town — "The fastest growing town in the west" — and there was much romance and human interest in the finding of it . . . unless you count the long days under the merciless sun, the desperate search for water with eyes almost glazed shut and the hunger for a kind word remembered from a boyhood in the shade back home.

The men responsible for Randsburg were three who had worked the scattered, played-out gulches around the fringes of the Mojave and had about given up ever making any big money. One was John Singleton, carpenter turned miner, who had gained much experience in the placers and hard rock mines but now was broke and discouraged. One was Frederick Mooers, clever newspaper writer but completely unfit to make a living, let alone a fortune. The third was Charles Austin Burcham, whose chief distinction was having a doctor for a wife. The total assets of the three were a team and wagon, bought with money Dr. Rose La Monte Burcham had earned delivering babies in San Bernardino.

JOSHUA TREES seem to form grotesque Conga line, posturing their way along sandy road in Red Rock Canyon. Several gold strikes brought series of rushes to gulches, leading into brilliant, eroded canyon. During one in 1893, prospector found $150 in four days, celebrated and returned with partner to take out $260 more. Tiny creek dried up and so did his hopes. Others, working on larger scale, did not depend on erratic stream flow, built "dry washers" operating on air blower principle. When all available gold was extracted prospectors left, to return when mountain storms formed Gully Washers in canyons. New beds of gold exposed, cycle started all over again.

Disgusted at finding no paying lode in Summit Gulch in 1895 — where Mooers and William Langdon had found some color earlier — the trio departed in the lumber wagon, heading for the hills where they spent a month until time and money ran short, as Burcham was nearing the end of a two-year limit imposed by his wife.

One night in April they made camp in a dry canyon not far from the Twenty Mule Team road between Death Valley and Mojave. The disheartened Mooers kicked his heels up the wash for fuel and gathered some greasewood stems when his eye caught a glint of yellow in a nearby ledge. Gasping, he dropped the brush and ran back for his pick. The first chunk of rock chipped off showed particles of gold all over it. "Boys!" he yelled, "we've struck it! There's no need to look any farther."

And for once the newspaper man made headlines with resounding effect. The three men secured eight claims and hired an expert quartz mining man to examine the ground, swearing him to secrecy. "You've got a good thing here," he reported. "Get a 100-stamp mill, shovel the whole mountain into it and your fortunes are made. The whole hill is good ore." Then he promptly broke the secret.

The news reached O. B. Stanton in Bakersfield who came running with cash. He liked what he saw and offered to spend $10,000 to get the mine started, erect a stamp mill etc., in return for one half interest. The agreement had the signatures of Mooers and Singleton but not Burcham. He was in Bakersfield giving his wife the good news and signing over to her half of his share, as agreed when she grubstaked him. "Now," Dr. Rose warned him, "don't you dare sign anything when you get back to the mine, at least until we know more about its value." Back at the mine Burcham was handed the document which he refused to sign. The deal fell through but the contract bearing the other two names would later be vital in endless and costly litigation.

Now here came the forthright doctor. In July she took charge of the mine situation while for the next several months the three men dug ore and crushed it by hand using a little water hauled from Cow Wells or Goler. Dr. Rose did the housekeeping and with blind faith of psychic assurance kept books while looking around for some way to finance and expand operations.

The partners got out enough ore to make two shipments to distant smelters in Montana. The rich ore was pulled down the mountain on sleds, transferred to wagons for hauling to Mojave and reloaded on flatcars. When the assay report came there was great rejoicing in camp and the four laid plans to begin mining on a larger scale.

SIDES OF RED ROCK CANYON are spectacularly eroded, giving effect of miniature Bryce. Harder rhyolite and sandstone of bright salmon-pink to red are moulded into fantastic forms, alternating with softer snowy-white clay in fluted columns. Canyon floor is composed of clean sand from walls, supports desert garden of cacti, "desert holly", greasewood, other shrubby growths, mostly prickly. One ampitheater-like area is filled with worshippers each Easter Sunday as first rays of sun enter gorge.

Meanwhile other mines were established — the Gold Coin, Napoleon, Bully Boy, Monkey Wrench, Wedge, Olympus, Trilby and King Solomon. One Swede miner called his claim The Big Norse. Si Drouillard found the rich St. Elmo, five miles from the original Rand, and this set off the big rush to Randsburg. Hopefuls from Los Angeles came as far as Mojave by train, boarding stages for Red Rock Canyon and Cow Wells where extra horses were hitched on for the steep stretch to Randsburg.

Every stage carried mail and a mixed assortment of humanity — miners, prospectors, legitimate business men who expected to open stores, as well as outcasts and riffraff from coast and eastern cities. Enough prostitutes, gamblers, pimps came along to populate a full-blown red light district, but gay and rowdy Randsburg never got a reputation for great violence. There were few killings as compared to those in other camps.

By 1897, Mooers, Singleton and Burcham had received something like $250,000 in payment for ore

RANDSBURG was built on whatever contour ground offered, one end of town much higher than the other. Main thoroughfare makes sharp hairpin curve into and out of town, following available levels. One comparatively level stretch, called Butte Street, intersected central business section. Building shown was famous Rinaldi's Market serving townspeople with meat and groceries over most of town's life.

DURING LUSTY DAYS, Randsburg's brothels were scattered among more reputable businesses, French Marguerite's exclusive bordello being immediately below Rinaldi's. Mothers, living still farther down gulch, forced to bring children past open doors often occupied by painted hussies, protested to civic authorities demanding that bawdy houses be segregated.

and their scraping days were over. Eventually revenues would amount to some $25 million from Randsburg mines. Legal disputes harassed the Rand mine, now called the Yellow Aster, some of them initiated by Mooers' former partner, William Langdon. He lost his case as did others who attacked the validity of the three partners' claims.

It was during this period that Daniel Kelsey struck it rich. A mule team driver, hauling borax for Coleman and Smith from the Harmony Works near Furnace Creek in Death Valley to Mojave, he quit the job because, as he said: "I just couldn't stand seeing those ornery critters go so long without water."

He made one trip with his own team, hauling lumber to the raw mining camp of Randsburg, stood enthralled in the midst of a thousand tents and a few board-and-canvas shacks, then bought some prospectors' tools and supplies. After a few weeks of fruitless picking and panning, he found some float in Yuma Canyon and tracked the ledge to its source. He chipped off a piece, showed it to a friend who invested $20,000 as a partner. The ledge started the famous Blue Daisy mine, which when sold for $170,000, sent the Dan Kelsey family on a grand tour of Europe.

Also during this period Pat Reddy finally gained what he had been refused in Randsburg's earlier days. Reddy was an attorney of sorts, self-educated and keen. He had never been admitted to the bar but made a reputation in the loosely conducted

courts of Nevada in the hectic '60s. In one scuffle at Aurora, he was wounded and eventually lost an arm. Reddy became state senator and then swung through the big mining camps where he fitted his talents into legal squabbles.

In Randsburg he approached the two-fisted Dr. Rose Burcham. "I tell you folks could do with a little cash to start things going," he said. "I'd be glad to advance say a few thousand dollars. Instead of repayment in cash, you can settle with me for a share of your mine." But Dr. B. was not about to see her project divided by even the smallest fraction no matter how much she needed money and no amount of pleading by Pat Reddy moved her. So smarting under the rebuff, he caught the next stage for Mojave.

When he later heard of the Yellow Aster's legal struggles, he hurried back and offered help. This time he found a desperate situation and his offer was accepted for a share of the mine. One phase of the case was won and Reddy's share eventually paid him enough to live on comfortably the rest of his life.

Over the years almost half the world's known minerals were found in the Rand and neighboring mountains. During the first years, if these were noticed at all, they were cast aside as worthless. Gold was all that mattered. But even the Rand's gold supply was not inexhaustible. When it thinned out and Randsburg's miners were scraping the bottom of the barrel, they found they had been overlooking real money in tungsten. In 1895 rich deposits of this element of the chromium family were found five miles from Randsburg, close enough to infuse new life into the fading camp, although the town of Atolia grew up on the immediate site, the name derived from the two men involved in early development, Atkins and De Golia.

With the World War demand for tungsten, excitement ran riot in the gulches, the metal being found mostly in placer deposits. This frantic activity produced in all $65 million worth. Men working in mines were searched and their lunchboxes examined at the portals, and as contraband ore continued to flow, miners were forced to change clothes after work. A shopping bag quickly filled with the ore, scheelite, would bring $350.

Then came the end of the war and almost complete collapse of the tungsten market. With gold mining tapered off at the Randsburg mines, the area went into another slump. The Yellow Aster was in the doldrums and by this time all three of the original partners were dead. Dr. Burcham still held her shares and Mooers' son Edwin retained a part, but law suits, strikes and other labor troubles had brought the famous old mine to a virtual standstill. One strike lasted sixteen years, brought to an end in 1918. With only a skeleton crew of three still employed there, much of the population of the once roistering, booming town had evaporated.

Then in 1919 came the discovery that a ridge of rock running down the slope of nearby Red Mountain was almost solid horn silver. Every former resident of Randsburg who could return to the dead town did so and again it served as in the tungsten boom. Two small centers sprang up close to the Big Silver, Osdick and Hampton, which were soon consolidated and ten years later given the formal post office name of Red Mountain. When the silver boom swelled to over $14 million in 1926, it showed signs of coming to an end. The mine was sold for $50,000 that year, the new owners doing nothing spectacular with it.

The Second World War made no stirring demand for tungsten and gold mining has made no comeback. Once again Randsburg has settled back on a comparative ghost town status. The inevitable tavern still operates, a desert museum is open on weekends displaying many of an almost endless variety of minerals and crystal specimens found in the surrounding hills. It is said of most dormant gold and silver mining towns that only a rise in prices of the metals would bring revival. In the case of Randsburg it would seem possible that one of the many minerals found hereabout and heretofore neglected, might suddenly become indispensable, causing history to repeat itself.

JOHANNESBURG, popularly Joburg, was less glamorous neighbor of Randsburg, contains few reminders of early days. It is busier today, being on highway, filled mostly with shanties and mobile homes. First houses were all frame, were destroyed by repeated fires. Later they were of adobe or as here, as scraps of tin or sheet iron — fireproof if not picturesque. Most prominent structure was 10-stamp mill, dominating town. One large hotel, boxy wooden structure, had about thirty-five rooms, was center of gay social events. Joburg also boasted several stores and saloons but no church, religious services sometimes held in school house.

GARLOCK, CALIFORNIA

The six mills in Garlock separated the gold from the ore hauled down from Randsburg and needed the water in the local wells. So did most of the few hundred souls in the camp. But there were those who scorned water like the plague and kept Cheney's Thirst Emporium in business . . . like "Lily of the Valley" who ran a one man hoisting operation at the bar, then roamed Garlock's street, crooning: "Oh, she's the lily of the valley, the bright and morning star".

A few desiccated cabins stood at the edge of the barren El Paso Range and the people who lived there paid $1 for a 52 gallon barrel of water. It would last the average family a week, with restraint on such things as laundering and dishwashing. Then some enterprising individual came to the cabins and dug a well. He was ridiculed . . . "Why anybody would know there isn't any underground water in an area where the annual rainfall is nothing minus." The digger was deaf to all this and found the water table at a depth of only 28 to 30 feet. He may have become a patron saint of the area which soon became a regular stopping place for prospectors and their wagons. And its name became Cow Wells.

Pioneer Robert Kelly wrote: "Plentiful water was necessary for the stock in the corrals. The large water tank was kept full by pumping with a large rotary contraption, pulled in a circular motion by a large, lazy black mule which needed constant prodding or he would go to sleep in his tracks. With sufficient urging he would stay on his job and pump a sufficient amount of water within a reasonable time to take care of the next day's needs. Then old Mule was turned back to his corral until his services were needed the next day . . . the tank also served for refrigeration in summer time, where my mother kept the butter, milk and other food."

These simple days came to an end with the need to mill the ores from the Rand mines. The poverty-plagued, discoverer-owners on Rand Mountain were determined to keep the mine "in the family" but even though the ores were extremely rich, it cost too much to ship it away for milling and it was out of the question to mill it on the spot as they had no water. Now with water at Cow Wells, a mill could be built there and ore hauled to it by wagon.

Eugene Garlock, always referred to as Gene, built the first — the Garlock Pioneer Mill — and the enlarged cluster of cabins took his name. A load of ore was driven down the grade from the Yellow Aster, at first called the Rand mine, and Dr. Bur-cham, the physician-wife of one of the partners. came with it to see that none of the ore was carried off — as it often was when shipments were piled around the mills, this taking of specimens termed a polite form of high-grading. The brick of gold resulting from the first milling was worth $800 and to Dr. Burcham fell the task of personally taking it to Mojave, as there was yet no Wells Fargo. She was nervous about bandits but did the best she could to conceal the brick under her skirt.

When the little Garlock Pioneer Mill proved inadequate to handle the increasing amounts of ore, five more were built — the McKernan, Kelley, Smith, Henry and Visalia. Gold was extracted by simple amalgamation, the ore not being refractory, and the power came from steam. Fuel was the big problem in this desert-type country. Brushy, twiggy, fast-burning branches had to do and it was fed to the fires with hay forks.

All ore was hauled by heavy wagons with broad iron tires to stay on top of the sand. The grade down from the Rand was steep with plenty of rough spots in the lower flats and deep washes. The wagons had to be eased down, then pulled by sheer horse or mule power.

The mule skinner's vocabulary is legendary, most drivers working a long string of vitriolic words to a high pitch of profanity as they lashed savagely with the whip. Little Joe did not believe in that kind of brutal treatment. When his team arrived at a bad gully, says Old Jim McGinn, who knew Little Joe in Garlock's good years from 1896 to 1899, he would walk around to the near lead animal, place his mouth close to the ear, whispering words of affection and encouragement. And he made the rounds, whispering in all the animals' ears. Then he got back in the driver's seat, picked up the lines and it never failed. At the signal the animals surged against their collars and took the load right out of the gully.

There were few buildings in Garlock but they made a break in the arid expanse. There was the Doty Hotel, a board and batten, two story structure. Another hotel was the Lilard, where the three daughters of the owner waited on table and later in the evening played the piano and sang for guests. Instead of tagging the girls with the usual "Faith, Hope and Charity", these were called "Tom, Dick and Harry".

The stable, or Big Barn, where horses on the Mojave-Randsburg run changed, was quite impos-

WEATHERED BUILDINGS—all that is left of once busy Garlock. At left is blacksmith shop, complete with forge; at right, livery stable — one end entirely closed for grain storage, rest of building open to weather on one side. Mountains in background are El Pasos, centered by El Paso Peak, 4,500 feet. Comparatively low range runs in east-west direction, is separated at western end from Kiavahs by Red Rock Canyon, scene of many early gold discoveries. Kiavahs, also a low range short distance north, ends at foothills of giant Sierra Nevada.

ing as were the McGinn Grocery, Lew Porter Store and the two saloons — Miller-Montgomery Bar and Cheney's Thirst Emporium. The first "postmaster" was Ida Kelly, wife of Kern County Constable John Kelly. Long after the demise of Garlock he would discover — by proxy — the famous Big Silver mine near Randsburg.

Garlock was fortunate to have a doctor all through its heyday — W. H. Wright. With his wife and three small children, Dr. Wright arrived by train and stage in 1896. One of the children, Sher-

man L. Wright now of Oakland, recalls those days: "The house which father constructed consisted of two rooms with lean-to at the rear. It was made of 1 x 12 inch boards nailed upright to a 2 x 4 framework. The total floor space was about 400 square feet. The front room was used as drug store, doctor's office, dental office and for general assembly of many miners. Later, about 1899 or 1900, half of this room was partitioned off for a post office which was operated until 1903 when it was abandoned for lack of business. The other room and

WELL PRESERVED REMAINS of arrastra include wooden parts, unrotted in dry desert air. Crude contraption crushed ore from mines of Randsburg before mills were built there. Ore, dumped unguarded around grinder, presented irresistable temptation to high-graders who claimed they were only selecting specimens. At first practice was condoned by mill owners but when samplers took to carrying off sacks full of jewelry rock, guard was posted.

lean-to were used for living quarters, kitchen, laundry etc., quite a common arrangement in those days.

"Aside from carrying on a general practice of medicine, my father practiced some dentistry consisting mainly of extracting and giving relief to aching teeth. I do not know that he did fillings or other repairs. In his spare time father was also a miner, preacher on Sundays and at funerals, Fourth of July orator, school board member, surveyor and self-constituted authority on anything. . . ."

The three children attended Garlock's little school. Desks were hand made, four feet wide, accommodating two pupils each. Girls were grouped on one side of the room, boys on the other. A wood-burning, cast iron stove stood in the center, gal-

vanized water pail and tin dipper near the front door. At the far end was a platform, teacher's desk and blackboard. The school doubled as church and meeting place for the Garlock Literary Society which was considered an "uplifting influence" to the town morals and a means of recognizing local talent at entertainments.

In the winter of 1897-98, a shadow fell on Garlock. A 28-mile railroad spur was completed to Johannesburg, connecting the Randsburg complex with the Atchison, Topeka and Santa Fe at Kramer. The line ran within a mile of the Yellow Aster and the mine could now ship ore to Barstow for more efficient milling. For a time some poor grade ore was still ground at Garlock, then a screw-pipe water

line was laid from the springs at Goler to Randsburg, making possible the construction of a 30-stamp mill right at the mines. When this was followed by a huge 100-stamp mill, the death knell of Garlock was sounded. The little school house, crowded to capacity during boom years, had only the three Wright children in 1902 and 1903.

"We remained at Garlock until 1903." says Sherman Wright, "by which time the population had dwindled to our family and a Mexican, Juan Barsarto, who took in washing. We abandoned our house and asked Juan to drive us in our four wheeler wagon to Mojave. We gave Juan the horse and wagon and took the train for Oakland. . ."

Garlock became a true ghost and except for an occasional tenancy by some wandering prospector, it remained completely deserted until 1911. In that year the Southern Pacific constructed a rail connection from Mojave to Keeler and crews camped in Garlock's weathered buildings. As rails extended they moved on and the little town was again empty.

Then in the early 1920s came a new resurgence. A salt company started mining the saline deposits of nearby Kane Lake. Mine owner and capitalist J. D. Voss and associates made a determined attempt to develop the old Apache mine in nearby Iron Canyon, and a new mining project took form at Mesquite Springs. There was a general occupancy of houses in Garlock, the need for a post office again, a new store was started by John Norton and a boarding house by Sarah "Granny" Slocum.

But ghosts would have the town. The salt project failed and the crew moved away. The men at the Apache mine folded their tents. No one asked for mail and the post office closed on June 30, 1926 — but who can say it was for the last time?

CENTRAL GEARS in museum-piece arrastra shows simple machinery. Turned by another gear operated by steam engine, central rod revolved, turning horizontal beams. Each of these was fastened to granite block, several shown here. These were dragged over ore thrown into pit, crushing it for gold extraction by amalgamation. Crude process wasted much gold, recovered later by mills in further processing by cyanide method, mine owners not sharing in salvage.

STONE STRUCTURE is only solid remnant of Garlock's buildings. Erected in 1897 by John Miller, it served primarily as stage depot but included bar operated by Miller and his partner Montgomery, and a store.

FRANKFORT, WASHINGTON

"Curiosity unveils marvels" and no one knows it better than Dr. Ralph Isaac of Portland, Oregon. He spends much time in the outdoors of his free days, eyes and ears open, feelers tuned to a sensitive pitch. One summer day in 1960 he and his son-in-law walked along the beach of the Columbia River, at Knappton on the north or Washington shore. The tide was going out and they looked for a trail to skirt the headland which appeared to block the way.

"We came to a group of weathered houses," the doctor told the author later, "some just above high water level, some well up the bank. At first we thought all the houses were vacant, although most of them were still furnished. We looked through one window into a kitchen and saw dishes and silverware still on the table, as if the people living there had just finished a meal. Exploring further we discovered the settlement wasn't entirely deserted, that it had two inhabitants, a German who lived alone at one end and a lonely Swede at the other. We talked to the latter, commenting it was fortunate he had company in the otherwise deserted place. His reply was: 'We got mad at each other a couple of years ago and ain't spoke since.'" Mindful of the returning tide which would block their return the two explorers were forced to leave, not relishing a climb over the intervening headland with its mantle of tangled vines and brush native to Washington's coastal regions.

Dr. Isaacs lead was tantalizing to this inquisitive photographer but—how to get to Frankfort with camera equipment when the light was right (all the buildings faced south and the Columbia) and not be at the mercy of ebbing and flowing tides? After several futile attempts to reach the spot, information came in the late summer of 1964 that the firm of Crown Zellerbach was logging on the bluff above Frankfort, that dirt roads had been knifed through the heavy timber to a point a mile above it. So an over-night camp was made and in the early morning a climb down an old overgrown trail.

Here was the classic deserted village—a small one almost isolated, never reached by road of any sort, without telephone, electricity or wheeled vehicle larger than a wheelbarrow. Frankfort's only exchange with the outside world was by fishing boats, the nearest towns mere settlements, the nearest city Astoria across the broad mouth of the Columbia River with its formidable bar and almost constant threat of storms. River traffic with Frankfort tied up at a wharf which extended out across the mud flats to deep river and which was now rotted and wrecked by heavy battering of waves, making Frankfort accessible only by small boats that could reach the bank at high water, or by foot. What was the story behind the desolation?

Early in 1890 two promoters, Frank Bourn and Frank Scott, took a long look at the small clearing they found on Gray's Bay. It seemed a likely spot to start a city, a river metropolis protected from fierce winter storms by a prominent headland. Maybe they could induce a railroad to build a line to the site or at least promise to. At any rate the two Franks could call their city Frankfort.

FRANKFORT RESIDENTS when Lawrence Barber visited isolated community in 1947. He found 11 people, 6 of them shown here. At left is Fred Hansen, who with 9 brothers and sisters, was raised in Frankfort, all attending one-room school presided over by teacher Ulrika Brandt, daughter of Swedish sea captain. She stands next in line, partly concealed by Hugo Claeson. Next is Mrs. Claeson, then Charles Lawrence and Mrs. Lawrence.

Rumors were soon spreading like wildfire, hinting that the Northern Pacific Railroad was actually surveying a route down the north bank of the Columbia to connect with ocean shipping points. Further, said the "overly Frank" reports, the line would pass directly along the edge of Gray's Bay, a station to be built where Bourn and Scott indicated.

The promoters built a flimsy landing float at the river's edge but its usefulness was limited, as lower reaches of the Columbia advance to the ocean only on the ebb tide, being forced backward on the flood. This meant that if prospective purchasers were dropped from boats on the wharf at low tide they were faced with a mile or more of oozy mud flats.

Yet buyers came on the heels of promises and the picturesque bay front seethed with activity. Bourn and Scott took in another partner, L. O. Chemault, and on May 15, 1890, filed the original plat of Frankfort, plans calling for 1226 lots. Streets and alleys were laid out with fine disregard of terrain, much of it swampy with only a narrow bench of solid ground, this terminating at the bottom of a steeply rising bluff.

Nevertheless many of the lots were sold. The promoters ploughed their increasing funds back into Frankfort's boggy soil, building a hotel, general store and sawmill, and all these signs of a city to be, encouraged more lot sales. A newspaper was soon in print, a saloon and then two more doing business. But it soon became apparent to the most

optimistic that with all this no railroad tracks were being laid. While a committee of inquiring citizens gathered at the front door of the real estate office, two of the partners faded away at the back, leaving Bourn to face the music.

Well, it was like this, he said—the railroad had decided against building the line. He had been informed of the change in plans only yesterday. However, nobody would regret his investing in the future of Frankfort. The site was perfect for a salmon cannery and think of that tremendous stand of timber at the very door of the sawmill. The committee went away and if its members were not placated, they grumbled without protest.

Bourn was still there ten years later when Axel Nelson arrived but the population had fallen to about 150. The salmon canneries were interested in Frankfort as Bourn had predicted but not to the extent of building plants. Two of the larger concerns, New England Fish Co. and Anderson Packing Co., had built substantial wharves where they could load fish netted by Frankfort fishermen and these companies had hired Nelson as agent to facilitate the buying and loading. He bought the long unused hotel built by Bourn and partners and rebuilt it as a substantial home.

At this time the *Mayflower, Pioneer, Julia B.* and other steamers plying the river made regular stops at Frankfort docks. When the *Mayflower* was condemned as unseaworthy she was replaced by the *Shamrock*. Five years later a smart new steamer, the *General George Washington* made its maiden voyage on the Columbia and began regular stops at Frankfort. The vessel had been built by its owners, William Anderson, Ed Simmons and Ed Shatto, was destined to be the most familiar steamer on the run, the best remembered by old timers.

Early in January, 1947, Lawrence Barber, marine editor of the Portland OREGONIAN, visited Frankfort and found only 11 residents, among them Axel Nelson. The community was even more isolated than in earlier days, having no mail delivery or regular boat service. Nelson complained that Frankfort was cut off from the rest of the world, that in case of emergency it had no way of getting word out. A man needing medical attention would die before any aid could be summoned. He said he had gone into the matter of getting the county to build a road, either from Knappton, a stretch of only three miles but over the steep intervening headland, or from Deep River to the north, three and a half miles over the mud flats. Either way the cost would be between $35,-

000 and $50,000 for a single lane graveled road and the county could not consider it.

Barber's story and pictures appeared in his newspaper January 12. On the 17th there was a news item from Astoria headed: "Navy To Help Isolated Area." The announcement read: "The navy Wednesday came to the rescue of Frankfort, Wash., the tiny community on the north shore of the Columbia." The item stated that Capt. L. B. Ard, commanding officer of the Tongue Point Naval Station would send a crash boat to Frankfort at the request of the Astoria Chamber of Commerce, and if any emergency condition was found to exist the navy would provide temporary weekly service until regular commercial boat service could be restored.

And a month later, on February 12, the OREGONIAN carried this dispatch: "Doctor Rushed To Isolated Area—The isolated community of Frankfort . . . called on the navy Sunday for assistance when one of its 12 inhabitants became suddenly ill. The navy command at Tongue Point dispatched a picket boat to carry Dr. J. B. Lund from Astoria to Frankfort to treat Leo Nelson who was seriously ill with intestinal influenza. . . . The navy has been sending a crash boat there occasionally as an emergency service."

Frankfort's ultimate usefulness was mentioned in the OREGONIAN's issue of January 14, 1953: "Logger Acquires River Townsite — The forest grown townsite of Frankfort, across the Columbia River from Astoria, has been sold at auction by Pacific County, Wash. for $74,918. E. J. Mell, Shelton, Wash. logger bought the bulk of the property . . . several independent buyers took lots on the waterfront that might be capable of development for resort purposes. The sale put an end to the dreams of real estate promoters of more than fifty years ago who platted the townsite in the hopes it would develop into the metropolis of the lower Columbia."

HOME OF AXEL NELSON, native of Finland, who arrived in Frankfort at turn of century. House was built of lumber salvaged from hotel made useless when plans for railroad collapsed. Most of furnishings remain, although badly damaged by vandals. Piano still stands in parlor but needle point settee dumped on front steps has been ruined further by rains which often total 15 inches a month in winter at near-ocean site. Moisture and mild climate foster heavy verdure which will soon engulf Nelson home and entire village.

VIEW FROM DESERTED VILLAGE of Frankfort across broad mouth of Columbia River. Early morning mists rise from water, partly obscuring Oregon coastal range in distance. Large public dock was wrecked in violent winter storm in 1933. Mud flats in center foreground are exposed by low tide which strongly affects Columbia here near ocean. Volume and power of water at flood are evidenced by stranded logs at shoreline.

LAST REMAINING RESIDENT of Frankfort was Swedish fisherman, Sven Hovic, who was taken to rest home in helpless condition in 1962. Sven had used most of his winter's wood, rest remaining to rot, as apples on tree. Wires were strung above fence to discourage marauding deer and elk, other residents using more effective fish net barricades 8-feet high.

KNAPPTON, WASHINGTON

Cement making started it, fishing and trapping added to its growth, sawmilling made it tick and fire put an end to everything—Knappton on the Columbia.

For two years, after the end of the Civil War, Job Lamley and George Hopkins lived alone on a narrow strip of land on the north shore of the Columbia River near its mouth. If they were not talking to each other, the arrival of six more people relieved the tension. The newcomers were R. N. Knapp and wife, their sons Amen and Jabez, Amen's wife and J. H. Burl.

Young Jabez was interested in minerals and geology, exploring the timber-covered hills that ran steeply up from the tiny settlement on the shore, and he found an outcropping of lime rock, a rarity in this predominately basaltic area. Experimenting with the material, he found it would make good cement and with partners Burl and Hopkins, started the small plant which gave the community its first name—Cementville.

The industry attracted workers, fishermen and trappers came to live there and a post office was established in 1871 with Jabez Knapp the first postmaster and the family name used in renaming the settlement. It soon became evident cement would not shape Knappton's future. The limestone rocks were being used up, outcropping confined to the surface, and the plant cut down operations.

Sawdust however was in the path of destiny. Flanked by a bountiful supply of virgin fir, spruce and cedar, the men who started the sawmill were sure it would succeed—Jabez Knapp, S. W. Backus, H. F. Williams, N. W. Spaulding and D. W. Grant, with James Vaughn hired to clear the land for the mill. Vaughn, born and raised in Keatesville, Missouri, enlisted in the Union Army with the Indiana

OLD KNAPPTON QUARANTINE STATION served 56 years. Four and a half acres of ground adjacent to docks site were logged off in 1899, wharf and buildings constructed same year, operations by U.S. Public Health Service started May 9th. Here were detained immigrants (mostly Orientals imported to work in New England Fish cannery) suspected of carrying communicable diseases. Fumigation of ships required two day period in early days when sulphur fumes were employed, operation being much expedited later with use of cyanide. Detained "guests" sometimes overflowing hospital buildings on wharf were accommodated in hull of old Navy cruiser Concord tied up alongside. Viewpoint here is western extremity of Gray's Bay, eastern arm shown in distance. Columbia River at this point is about seven miles wide.

Volunteers and at the end of the war came northwest to Old Chinook at Point Ellice near Knappton to fish for salmon. Between fish runs he worked at the cement plant, displaying an eagerness and ability for the land clearing job.

Engaged also by the sawmill company to build the mill was craftsman Samuel Everhart Barr, Pennsylvania born and migrant to Portland, Oregon, in 1859. Like Vaughn, Barr brought a young wife with him and the two families built a house to occupy jointly. It had a common kitchen with a board across the center, used to separate warring factions among the rapidly growing brood of children when they were less than amicable.

James Vaughn became chief log supplier for the mill. Close in timber had been cut for building of stores and houses but an almost limitless supply of trees extended in three directions from the river. Vaughn had homesteaded a 160-acre tract of timber at the mouth of near by Deep River and now with twelve men and eight yoke of oxen, he became one of the first "contract" loggers in the area. Some of the first trees could be felled directly into the river and rafted to the mill. As the stand receded from shore, short skid roads were laid down, oxen dragging the big logs from woods to river.

Until 1875 the Knapp family was predominant in the town, then a commanding figure appeared — Asa M. Simpson. He was a Maine man, born February 21, 1826 in New Brunswick, apprenticed to a shipbuilder at 14. On his tenth birthday his father gave him a one-thirty-second interest in the four-masted bark *Birmingham* and at 23 he shipped as her supercargo, sailing around the Horn and arriving in San Francisco in the midst

of gold fever in 1850. Going directly to the gold fields, Asa made a small strike and with New England frugality invested it in the ship *H. F. Gray*, first ship built in San Francisco Bay. Later the ship was lost and so was Simpson's money.

Then he persuaded the owners of the *Birmingham* to haul lumber to Stockton, the venture recouping his small fortune. He bought a share in the *Potomac* but this ship was disabled and nearly wrecked off the Columbia River in 1852. While waiting for her to be repaired in Astoria, he built a sawmill only to have it lost in a sudden business depression. With what money he had left he bought into the ship *Harriet* and began hauling lumber down the coast. While at the mouth of the Umpqua River, awaiting a cargo of piling, he heard Indian tales of the immense stand of timber around Coos Bay and made an overland trip to see for himself. This area supplied the nucleus of his later successes, providing cargo for his ships.

That year, 1875, he built the first full-rigged ship launched on the Pacific Coast, *Western Shore,* at his shipyard in North Bend, Oregon. It was on her maiden voyage to Knappton for lumber that Asa Simpson recognized the possibilities in the little sawmill. He bought it — lock, stock and barrel — installing Melville P. Callendar as superintendent. "For the next thirty years," relates Carlton E. Apello of Deep River, local historian, "The Callendars, Melville and Charlie, ran the mill."

It was the only important industry in a remote, almost isolated area and had a strong impact on people in surrounding villages — Deep River, Salmon Creek, Frankfort, Crooked Creek, Naselle and Grays River — which depended on the lumber activity as well as fishing and farming. When winter stopped normal ways of making a living, many

ROTTING BONES of partially constructed 120' vessel lie in muddy slough near Knappton. One story says wreck is that of transport ship floated off the ways at Columbia City by flood waters during World War I, winding up on beach many miles down river, that end of war precluded salvage. Better substantiated is information supplied by merchant-historian Carlton Appelo, Deep River. He says that a Mr. Callendar of Knappton purchased half-built boat from shipyard at Astoria with intention of finishing it for own use, abandoned project when it proved impractical and too costly. Situation of derelict was once exposed to open river, now is enclosed by dike carrying modern highway, water still ebbs and flows with tides and seasons through culvert under dike.

DEEP RIVER, Washington, looks much as it did in early days when loggers gambled wages away in saloon of Shamrock Hotel, right. Building went up in 1900 as store with living quarters above, built by Charles Schwegler whose father, Christian, came from Germany to Deep River as homesteader about 1862. Structure was remodeled into saloon, hotel upstairs, by new owner Mr. Reikkola in 1904.

Activity began when Bell Logging Co. cut nearby timber, hauled logs to dump by ox teams. By 1898 Olsen Brothers had taken over, found trees too far back to haul on skid road, built first logging railroad in area. All logs were floated to Knappton Sawmill until it burned. Deep River Timber Co. built booming grounds in late 1920s, were able to raft 450,000 board feet per day in logs worth $19,000.

men moved their families to Knappton and went to work in the mill.

Ships from all nations called at Knappton for lumber, one of them, the *Rival,* American bark of 299 tons. At Knappton the vessel took on hay, lumber and shingles in September of 1881. Like hundreds of ships before and since, the *Rival* stranded on Peacock Spit, notorious sand bar at the Columbia mouth called the "Graveyard of the Pacific." Caught in a dying wind while on the bar, then driven onto the spit by a change in the wind with both anchors dragging, the hull ploughed into the sands. The tug *Astoria* managed to get a line on her but the hawser snapped. The storm swung the vessel completely around, breaking the anchor chain and carrying the *Rival* high on the beach between Cape Disappointment and McKen-

zie Head. Her master, Capt. Thomas B. Adams, wife, and crew, took to the boats which careened on the beach but landing all safely. The $8,000 bark and $6,000 cargo were a total loss.

On Saturday, July 12, 1941, the Knappton mill which had served the town for seventy years, burned to the ground and pilings. The blaze started in the planing mill, destroying a million feet of dressed lumber. Casper Korpela, working atop the refuse burner, was able to get down and make his escape only a few feet ahead of the flames. Burned were the main mill buildings, office, oil house and yard office. In its early stages the fire ate through the wooden water main, draining storage tanks so fire fighters were completely helpless.

Coast Guard lighthouse tender *Manzanita* crossed the Columbia from Astoria to ply water

33

on the flames, saving some lumber on the wharf and a portion of the wharf itself. Two barges loaded with 9 million feet of lumber were saved as were two automobiles driven onto the stacked lumber.

And the town of Knappton died, too. Eighty-five permanent jobs were wiped out and the post office closed November 15, 1943. Abandoned homes and the few buildings remaining from the holocaust began to weather and collapse. In 1960 a new state highway slashed through the nearly deserted site, eliminating most evidence of what had been Knappton. Today the old quarantine station buildings remain on their wharves, as does a tiny cluster of gray, weathered houses. At the river's edge are the stubby pilings, concrete and brick foundations of the huge boilers that once generated steam to power the screaming saws of the Knappton mill.

PADDY McGOWAN from the Auld Sod, later from Portland, Oregon, came to the north shore of Columbia river where it enters Pacific Ocean in 1852. He established a thriving business of catching and salting salmon for foreign shipment. Indians from nearby settlement of Chinook made temporary tent village at fishing site, returning home in winter. Paddy built first salmon cannery on lower river, operated at first by Indian help. He married New York girl, Jane Huntley, had four sons, one of them Henry Silas marrying and continuing to live nearby. Henry's widow, now 92, still resides in this almost vanished community named for father-in-law. Ornament draped from window is string of "corks," fishing net floats referred to in sketch of Wauna, Oregon.

ALTOONA, WASHINGTON

If you were a salmon fisherman living in Altoona, mused a newspaper reporter, on the north shore of the Columbia River near it mouth, you would be one of a hardy breed. You rode out into that turbulent, treacherous river, usually out over the bar where she spreads murkily into the heaving Pacific and where a storm can blow up like the temper of a shrew. You tossed out your small gill net and staked your life on the catch. It was a hard life but a glad one and you didn't complain. But the going got really tough when that old devil river choked herself on ice and your isolated village was cut off from the outside world for two weeks and you got so hungry you could eat your oilskins.

The Portland OREGONIAN of January 23, 1930 carried a dramatic story of relief for the near-starving residents of Altoona. The whole Pacific Northwest shivered in below zero temperatures for thirteen days, the worst weather in forty years. Even the lower Columbia region, usually subject to no more cold than occasional frosts, was in deep freeze with temperatures as low as 10 above, and the river was covered with an unbroken crust of ice.

Altoona, like several other communities on the river with no roads, depending entirely on water traffic, began to get hungry when boats did not dock. Then on the 21st a freezing rain started to fall, soon coating wires with ice, the weight of it threatening to ground the single telephone line to the outside. Before it came down the people sent out a distress call which got to Astoria, Oregon, across the river.

Next day the Arrow Tug and Barge Co. of Astoria dispatched a sturdy tug loaded with food. It broke ice successfully in the faster running channel but was unable to get nearer than 350 feet from the North Shore. So the hungry Altoonans walked out on the ice to where the supplies were dumped from the tug, five of them fighting the numbing cold river water to get aboard the vessel, wanting to see Altoona never again. The others worked their way back and the emergency was relieved.

Pillar Rock in the Columbia River just east of Altoona, is an historic landmark around which much of the lower river activity has centered. A rugged column rising some twenty feet above deep channel water level, it was noted by British explorer Lt. William Robert Broughton in 1792 when he sailed up to it in the armed tender *Chatham* and commented it was "a remarkable pillar of rock." Later Lewis and Clark made notes about the rock in their journal.

Around 1840 the Hudson's Bay Co. established a salmon barreling operation near Pillar Rock and the local Chinook Indians caught salmon in their

WAHKIAKUM COUNTY COMMUNITY of Altoona was largely built on docks. Pilings supported huge cannery operations, space for drying and repairing nets, segregated housing for Chinese workers and general store, Altoona Mercantile. Closed for many years, store was last operated by W. L. Smith who turned to fishing. Cavernous cannery buildings sit on more solid section of same wharf.

COVERED BRIDGE over Gray's River close to mouth at Gray's Bay, is unique in having no windows. Gravels of stream yield agates and rock specimens especially after spring freshets.

willow weirs and nets, packing them down with salt, sailing vessels loading the barrels as cargo for London. Ships heading upriver to Vancouver would tie up at the rock to wait for favorable winds and tides. The respite from a long voyage was so welcome to the sailors they usually ended the breather with black eyes and broken noses in brawls over the Indian women fish packers.

In the 1870s a large fish cannery was operating just west of the Pillar, the locality called Altoona. In expanding its activities at the river mouth, the New England Fish Co. took over the cannery and enlarged it. For several years large numbers of Chinese were imported to gut and clean the salmon, their usefulness ending with the introduction of the Iron Chink, mechanical marvel that did all the cleaning and cutting.

As salmon runs diminished and canning became unprofitable, the company changed over to fish oil reduction and then in the late '40s closed down entirely. During these busy years the hamlets of Altoona and Pillar Rock were accessible only by boat, no great handicap when hundreds of gill netters swarmed the river and steamers made regular stops. But with the cannery closed, boats fewer and river steamers no longer running, the communities were cut off from the world. It was not until the early 1950s that a road was cut through to them — to all but Brookfield. The cannery there burned and the deserted town never did get more than a rough dirt track through the

timber. It is now used as a log dump by Crown Zellerbach, access not available to the public.

Just off Altoona Head, rocky point projecting from shore at the western edge of the village, lies the wreckage of the British steamer Welsh Prince. At 11:10 P.M. on May 28, 1922, she met the American freighter Iowan head on in a grinding collision. In the dense fog common to the lower river, neither vessel could see the other even after the crash until the British ship sent up an orange flare which showed her to be on fire. Her fore quarters were nearly severed, seven seamen crushed to death and she was settling fast. Responding to distress signals, the Oneonta set out from Astoria, feeling her way through the fog and removing the bodies of five men, two trapped in the sinking forecastle.

When the vessels were separated it was found that the Iowan could be towed even with her crushed bow and she was taken to Portland for repairs. When the fog cleared the upper decks of the Welsh Prince could be seen just above the water as she settled to the bottom. After several attempts to raise her, agents Frank Waterhouse and Co. notified the Furness Line of London that their ship was a total loss.

In that position close to the main channel, the hulk was declared a menace to navigation and M. Barde and Sons were employed to break it up. The firm brought ten tons of super-power gelatin dynamite from Olympia, Washington, blew off the top deck, then blasted the hull apart.

VADER, WASHINGTON

Vader, in the heart of the great Washington logging area south of Olympia, where Swedes and Finns and bull teams were trying to "get daylight into the swamp," had its share of shooting scrapes and murders. But while old-timers, including keen-minded Norman "Pat" Hitchcock, have trouble recalling the full details of them, sharp and clear is the memory of Husky Dog. Everyone who lived in Vader around 1906 will tell you about the town's most proficient alcoholic.

George Gale, now of Olympia, heard the story from Bill Dickenson who lived in Vader for several years. Husky Dog was brought down from Alaska by some prospector who wandered on, leaving his sled dog as a public charge. Bill Dickenson adopted the animal and always took him along when he had one or two in Vader's several bars. One evening as he stood up to the bar in the Spangler Hotel, Bill thought Husky Dog might be thirsty too, ordered an extra glass of beer and set it on the floor. Husky Dog sniffed but turned his head until a little of the brew was poured on the floor. He eagerly lapped up the sample and the rest in the glass when it was poured out. The husky's several admirers "set 'em up" for him all evening and when Bill left the dog walked as he never had at "40 below in the Arctic snow."

The next evening bartender Pat Hitchcock opened up and who but Husky Dog was waiting

VADER'S OLD CITY HALL is crowded by trees, grass, brush. At left are council chambers and shown under cedar tree barred windows of two-cell jail. Most occupants of hoosegow were drunks but it also held murderers. At right is fire station once sheltering two-wheeled hosecart pulled by hand by volunteer fire-laddies, sometimes in 4th of July parades. Hose-drying tower was surmounted by belfry, fire bell weighing more than 800 pounds. Present Vader resident John Groleau remembers when supporting timbers were judged unsafe and bell was removed. He says: "We attached ropes to it and pulled. It made a big crash when it came down, the belfry along with it. It landed behind the building. We always intended getting it out on the main street and mounting it some way as a momento, but never did."

OLD VADER HOTEL, last one to go and was under wrecking hammer when photo was made in 1962. Vader had at least five saloons, two housed in hotels. Near this building was newspaper office where GAZETTE was published.

at the door. Pat poured him a drink on the floor before serving anyone else, recognizing the hangover. The dog stayed in the bar all evening and when it closed he had to be ejected — but not like the men. The "cork-booted" inebriates had to be helped or carried out but Husky Dog was cooperation itself, letting himself be gently guided out. Then his aplomb deserted him. He headed for Bill's cabin but collapsed beside the road to sleep it off.

And so in truth Husky Dog became the furry face on the barroom floor, his progress downward being rapid because of an amiable nature that could not say "no." Several years of guzzling, says George Gale, "soon ruined Husky Dog's beautiful physique, turning him into a 300-pound monster with a gut like a beer barrel. His meaty jowls meas-

ured 24 inches from ear to ear. He became famous as the only dog in the country who could smile" . . . and that was about all. When forced to leave any bar at 2 a.m. he usually tried to make it to the nearby livery stable or blacksmith shop, Bill's cabin having long proved out of range. If he fell short of either he simply slept there, carrying his own blanket against the coldest weather.

And alas, retribution reaped its reward—Husky Dog fell seriously ill. His many friends came to his aid, guaranteeing care by the local doctor who immediately placed his patient on the water wagon. The dog lived a few months, then died in his sleep. Again quoting George Gale: "For Husky Dog the cork had been pulled, the bung knocked out of the barrel."

In the early 1850s flat-bottomed boats nego-

NEAR NEIGHBOR was town of Olequa, named for nearby stream. Was mostly farming community, depending largely on production of hops. With increasing expense of growing and lessening demand for hops, industry declined, most residents moving away. At one time several buildings stood at crossroads, center of Olequa, grocery store last to go. This photographer found only ruins of recently wrecked structure, settled for only remaining evidence of Olequa's one-time lively industry, fast-decaying hop drier.

tiated the Cowlitz River as far as Toledo, a land route, "military road," roughly paralleling the waterway. Near the small falls on Olequa Creek, a Cowlitz tributary and conveniently near the highway, the small village of Little Falls came into existence by the early 1880s, thought to be an outgrowth of an earlier Indian village, with post office, one-room school, general store, hotel and several houses.

When the Northern Pacific Railroad came this way it stopped not at the hamlet but at a point about a mile south, advancing no reason for naming the stop Sopenah. One old-timer in the area says a shipment of soap addressed to the general store in Little Falls, Wash., was sent instead to Little Falls, Minn., and the railroad wanted no more such mistakes. In any event, for many years mail came to the town addressed "Little Falls," rail shipments tagged "Sopenah."

Businesses found it more convenient to move closer to the rail point where others were already established, and took the Little Falls name along with them, the station alone retaining the word Sopenah. The community boomed in the latter part of the century, one large industry the Little Falls fire clay factory, using local high quality clays, and the Stillwater Logging and Lumber Co. Several hotels did a thriving business — Bannon, Spangler, Stillwater, the latter a three-story structure as was the school house. The town was also proud of its Opera House where thespians emoted from the heart to audiences of the bustling metropolis, then the busiest between Portland and Tacoma.

Among employees in the Stillwater mill was a Kentuckian. He liked his job on the edger so well and wrote home so glowingly many of his friends in the Blue Grass State joined him, resulting in a formation of a clique at the plant. Member stood by member on any and all occasions, as the time one of the southerners got into a quarrel with Ed Bertrand in one of the saloons. The two exchanged a few blows, the man from Kentucky getting the worst of it. He backed out the door vowing to get even, borrowed a gun at a friend's house, returned to shoot point-blank at Bertrand.

The killer waited for trial in the City Hall jail, facing almost certain conviction since the shooting had been witnessed by many. But his fellow Kentuckians collected a purse large enough to hire a clever lawyer to defend the prisoner. At the trial, self-defense was claimed with the contention that Bertrand attacked first, was even wearing brass knuckles. The accused was acquitted and released.

During Little Falls' best years there was continuing argument about the name of the town and station, railroad steadfastly refusing to conform. Finally a conference between townsmen and railroad officials brought the positive promise that the line would change the name, but not to Little Falls. So citizens huddled at City Hall and decided to call the town after a long time resident—Mr. Vader. The railroad went along with that.

Vader is today a near ghost. Gone are the hotels, saloons, industries. Quiet streets see little movement — of live people, that is.

39

MAYGER, OREGON, had large store built on pilings over river. This is now discontinued but gas station for passing fishing and other boats still functions. Around turn of century Mayger was busy, had large docks piled high with cordwood for fueling river steamers, later supplied wood for fueling locomotives, first one being No. 7. Much freight marked for surrounding logging camps came to Mayger, was then freighted to destination in deep timber by wagon. Community was also home and headquarters for many salmon fishermen. One was John Bryant who arrived in Mayger with family in 1896, spent 14 years fishing salmon, then passed away at family home. Two sons still make their living by fishing — Ralph at Astoria, William at Longview, Wash.

WAUNA, OREGON

The primary worth of Wauna was measured in sawn lumber but along with this went the manufacture of corks. Since commercial cork is a product of Spain, Portugal and Africa, what was it doing in a backwater area of the lower Columbia River? The explanation lies in the fact that these corks were of red cedar, the best floats fishermen could use for their nets.

"Wauna is an Indian name," writes Lewis M. McArthur, authority on Oregon place names, "probably Klickitat. It describes a mythological being who was supposed to represent the Columbia River." There was an Indian village on the site of Wauna but one white man's activity began with the Joe Berglund business of lathe-turned corks.

Gill nets are lead-weighted along the bottom rope, the upper line kept near the surface of the water by oval-shaped wooden floats about 8 inches long—the corks. In Pacific Northwest waters they are invariably made of the local red cedar for prime lasting qualities when water-soaked. With holes drilled lengthwise, they are strung along the line like big beads, tied about 2 feet apart. In the heyday of gill netting on the Columbia there was always a demand for the corks and Joe Berglund decided to make some extra money by setting up a lathe and turning out some for his fellow fishermen.

A former logger in the Ostrander camp near Kelso, then the Portland camp, both in Washington, Berglund moved his fish nets and equipment into a three-room houseboat which he moored at a point on the Columbia known as Cape Horn, then later to Mount Coffin, a rocky promontory on the river so named for the many Indian burials on its summit. It was near the tiny settlement of LaDu, and both rock and community would be included in the site of Longview. In Joe Berglund's family were a boy Kenneth and daughter Doris. (Kenneth was born in Portland at the home of his father's sister, Nanny Florin, author's mother — Editor).

The Berglunds started their cork business in rented buildings but in 1914 when Long-Bell Lumber Co. took over the area for Longview, they loaded all their belongings in the houseboat and moved to a 13-acre parcel they had bought a mile from Wauna where a sawmill had been started by the O. K. Logging Co. two years earlier.

The Berglund "farm" extended from the edge of Wauna Slough which was inundated each spring by high water in the Columbia and high ocean tides. But on this tidal flat stood a rocky knoll which afforded good dry land perch for the houseboat and allowed a small mill to be built at the water's edge where fishermen could tie up their boats and load the corks they bought. A gasoline engine ran the mill and lathe. If the tide was high visitors by land were forced to wait at the gate, and shout for someone to row over for them. Meanwhile Elin Berglund hastily tidied up her house. Every summer an elevated board walk was built as a bridge but spring freshets always carried it away.

After a few years a new house was built higher on the hill near the highway, but before it was completed the exhouseboat remained home and shop for the cork operations. Waterproofing with Valdura was considered necessary, the corks hand-rubbed with the liquid which was kept warm on a low-burning Primus gasoline stove. Kenneth was old enough to help his father, handing him the corks to be rubbed, then racking them for air-drying. On one fatal day, when the black waterproofing liquid was running low, Joe Berglund filled up the pot. A few drops splashed into the burner—and in an instant flames were spreading in all directions.

In a near-panic, Joe headed for the kitchen door at the west end of the house but found the door latched on the outside. Smashing his fist through the glass to reach the knob outside, he gashed his arm badly above the wrist. Outside he looked for

LARGE SAWMILL, devastated by floods and freezing weather, hampered by increasing lack of suitable logs, limped along until 1958. Small planing mill nearby operated until 1962. Actual wrecking had not started when this photo was made but deterioration is evident.

MAIN STREET of central part of Wauna. Camps for Greek and Japanese workers were separated under a modified caste system. Some pre-wrecking salvage operations were being started when photo was made.

TWO-ROOM SCHOOL HOUSE for lower grades where three Berglund children, Kenneth, Doris and Frank were pupils. Single room school nearby took upper graders. The late Willard Evenson of Wauna Lumber Co. sponsored a 12-boy basketball team which never won a game but was politely invited to a league tournament and surprised everyone including p'ayers and most of all, Coach Ned Shaw, by taking first place.

HAPPY GROUP of wild blackberry pickers photographed near Wauna in 1929. Clockwise young people are: Margaret Karlquist, Einar Karlquist, Frank Berglund, Roy Karlquist, author Lambert Florin, Kenneth Berglund (with blond hair) and Doris Berglund — all brothers, sisters or cousins.

Kenneth, found he had escaped through a rear window, but his hands were badly burned, his nails crisped.

Together they ran to the home of a neighbor, Bert Laws, leaving a trail of blood on the snow. Laws bound Joe's arm with a makeshift tourniquet, ran out to the road and stopped the first car that came along. The driver was a Japanese sawmill worker and since his people were ostracized by most of the whites, it was only after strong persuasion and some threats he agreed to help, by driving the Berglunds to the doctor at Westport. But while Joe's arm was cared for and Kenneth's burns dressed, the land-fast houseboat burned to the ground and with it many of the family's possessions.

Kenneth, his sister Doris, brother Frank, and later youngest brother Benny attended classes in the two-room schoolhouse in Wauna, one room for the first three grades, the other for fourth and fifth. Next door was a one-room school for the sixth, seventh and eighth grades.

When Kenneth finished school he worked at odd jobs and helped his folks improve the home place. One project was to cut out a stand of alder trees and buck them up for wood. At this work the twenty-two year old caught a heavy cold which turned into rheumatic fever and Kenneth died a short time later in a hospital. His funeral was held in the Wauna Community Hall, the building crowded with most of Wauna's population.

The Columbia Valley Lumber Company operated a big cargo mill in Wauna until 1911 when the Crosset-Western Lumber Co. purchased it, sawing old growth yellow fir and spruce from northwestern Oregon forests and loading it aboard steam schooners for Australia, China, Japan and the Atlantic Coast.

Crosset-Western employed 300 men at the Wauna mill, sawing logs from the Big Creek area toward Astoria, producing 60 million feet of lumber annually. Except for a brief shut down during "the depression," the mill continued in operation until 1941 when it was sold to the Evenson-Allen family of Clatskanie. As the Wauna Lumber Co. with about 185 employees, the mill ran until 1958 when obsolete equipment and the economics of the times forced a final closing. A small remanufacturing plant and planer mill used the site for a time, keeping about 30 men on the payroll until it closed in 1961.

A year later the giant Crown-Zellerbach Company purchased the entire site of some 1,000 acres. In the fall of 1962 the concern made it known that all buildings, residences, school, stores and hall would be razed along with the huge mill, all homes to be vacated by July 1, 1963. In April of 1964 plans were announced for a $15 million paper mill to be built at the location.

The old Wauna was dead but in its place would be a new Wauna to prosper on pulp wood rafted in huge quantities from points all along the Columbia.

WAUNA COMMUNITY HALL was center of joyful and sad gatherings. Funeral services were held here for twenty-two year old Kenneth Berglund who lived in Wauna almost all his life.

COMPANY STORE carried almost everything sawmill workers and families might want, supplies for neighboring population of fishermen, mostly gill netters. Combination store, offices and post office were erected fall of 1910. Mrs. Celia Smith, now of Portland, went to Wauna in 1941, her husband having taken job in mill. Three years later she became acting postmaster, then with a commission in 1948, served until closure of office in June, 1963.

HISTORIC OLD HOUSE was built, in part at least, in 1888 by William L. Brown in Apiary, now nearly vanished. It was named for beehives of early resident David M. Dorsey. William Brown had married Irene Lowman in Olive Hill, Kentucky, in 1885, and the couple came to nearby Rainier in 1887, taking homestead claim the next summer. When house was built, the Browns had one child, their first one having died earlier. In house shown thirteen more children were born to them, eight sons and five daughters. The father died here in 1932 and until 1964 the house was still occupied by a bachelor son.

ABANDONED SCHOOL in town of Natal, on Nehalem river between Mist and Pittsburg. Nathaniel C. Dale settled here in early '70s. He had to go to Mist for mail and as others settled near him, he brought their mail also. When community grew large enough for name residents honored him by using contraction of his given name. Natal got its own post office Oct. 2, 1899 with Roderick C. Cole as postmaster. After five years patronage loss, office was discontinued.

NEW ERA, OREGON

New Era. The name held promise, hope. Maybe, thought Joseph Parrott, that would be just the name for the community springing up around his store and grist mill on Parrott Creek flowing into the Willamette River above the falls. It was the name of the religious group on the hill overlooking the farm he settled on in 1855 — The New Era Spiritualist Society which printed a little tract, THE NEW ERA. Maybe with the railroad coming now in 1869, the settlement would be inspired with that name — New Era.

In 1892 a five-year-old girl saw this new land with big, wondering eyes. Now Laura Ellen Thompson, she looks into the past when her father turned his back on the wild and wicked mining country around Dillon, Montana, and brought his family to the mild climate and rich soil of Oregon.

As activities of the spiritualist society broadened its members acquired more land and buildings, starting a regular summer program of camp meetings. They must have been very successful, Laura believes, as she remembers "long lines of wagons full of people waiting to buy tickets for camping privileges. We attended some meetings although my folks never actually joined. They were very interesting, stressing the return of one's spirit after death."

By this time the little store of Joseph Parrott was inadequate and outdated. Laura's father saw his

OLD HERMAN ANTHONY FARM on hill above railroad, across from grounds of New Era Spiritualist Church and campgrounds, half-mile from site of Catholic Church and cemetery, Anthony, immigrant from Germany, was familiar with "Lichgate" (old English "Lychgaet") and decided one could well serve as portal to his farm. This type of gate had a somber origin in Europe, was covered entrance to burial grounds where preliminary services were held at bier. Cupolas and other old world touches adorn old outbuildings dating from about 1880. Anthony was enthusiastic beekeeper, had own ideas about care, such as large bee house to shelter hives in winter, not successful in mild Oregon climate. Bee house is still intact as are other structures, livery stable at right now serving as garage.

opportunity and built a larger one beside the road paralleling the river and railroad tracks. He was appointed postmaster and at one side of the store the Wells Fargo Company had its offices. His daughter says: "There was a great deal going on all the time. Father would be selling groceries, weighing postal parcels and relieving the Wells Fargo man all at the same time."

The valley soil was every bit as rich as newcomers expected — black, loamy stuff that grew great quantities of top quality potatoes. The farmers soon were growing more of them than could be consumed locally and shipped them to Portland. Because of the falls at Oregon City, the crop was hauled in wagons to that point, transferred to boats below the falls. After a system of locks was built, boats could load at New Era and when the railroad came through, produce was shipped by train.

A year after Laura's arrival at New Era she started school in the little one room schoolhouse which taught all grades. Another pupil was a boy of her age, John Thompson. They grew up with an "understanding" and when John got a job on the river steamer IRALDA, which plied the Columbia River with terminal dock at Rainier, Oregon, John moved there. He did not see much of Laura for a while, only on trips to New Era with his parents.

They were both eighteen on one of these trips and were married. John went to work for the railroad and the couple moved to Portland. He was with the railroad the rest of his working years, eventually retiring with Laura to a home on the banks of the Willamette near Milwaukie, not far from their old New Era haunts.

ANCIENT CATALPA TREE towers over Anthony farmhouse, second on site, built around 1890. Other lofty trees such as birchers at right surround old house, now home of James Stoltzer family.

LITTLE FALSE-FRONTED GEM in picture made about ten years ago, torn down in August of 1964. It had distinction of once being Wells Fargo station as well as containing general store and post office.

MASONRY DAM, fully 100 years old, has withstood ravages of time, pressure of water and roots of trees growing on it. Thickly covered with moss and "licorice" ferns, it is further screened from busy highway by alder trees and relic's existence is unrealized by most travelers. A sizeable pond is impounded behind dam, edges fringed with cattails, rushes. Sluice gate is partially choked where full rush of water once ran thru penstock to power wheel of grist mill. Now on private property, mill is shambles of rotting lumber, machinery. Swordfern fronds in foreground remain all winter. New crop will come up in early spring, making large clump. Almost impenetrable tangle of brush in background is typical of most logged-off hills in western Oregon.

COMPLETION OF OREGON AND CALIFORNIA RAILWAY to New Era from Portland, distance of twenty miles, on Dec. 24, 1869, was great event. To celebrate, excursion party crowded cars on Dec. 30 for special trip to young town beside Willamette River. Fire wood for engine was carried in little car behind locomotive. Small trees in background are second growth Douglas firs such as those serving as Christmas trees shipped all over country.

WHEN CATHOLIC CHURCH WAS BUILT priest planted two tiny poplar cuttings, one at each side of front door. Church is now long gone put poplars are enormous.

AURORA, OREGON

If Cheyenne Chief Shot In The Hand saw the desert cavalcade he must have said to his medicine man in whatever way he said things to his medicine man — "Well, old herbs and skulls, I've seen everything now." Yet whatever the Indians did think of this "far out" procession on the Oregon Trail, they let it alone. Dr. Wilhelm Keil had a safety factor working for him.

The outfit would have startled any good honest settler. Leading the string of covered wagons were two mules pulling a hearse, inside it a lead-lined casket filled with alcohol in which was preserved the body of a nineteen-year-old boy. Beside the hearse rode several German band musicians playing doleful Teutonic hymns which were sung by others riding behind. Then followed the wagons with women and children and supplies of a large party head-ing for the Willamette Valley. This was the wagon train of the fanatical religious leader, Dr. Wilhelm Keil and his followers.

Born in Bleicherod, District of Erfurt, Prussia on March 6, 1812, young Keil emigrated to the new world in 1836. Tailor by trade, he worked in a New York clothing factory and being diligent he would have done well but for his constant exhortations on religion among his fellow workers. They protested and Keil was discharged. German Methodism now took over his whole being and moving to Pittsburgh, he was ordained a Methodist preacher.

For a time dispensing gospel in the conventional manner satisfied his zeal but soon his radical tendencies set him in open revolt and he cut himself off from his church and moved to Shelby County, Missouri, where in 1845 he formed a colony of sym-

DR. WILHELM KEIL BUILT HUGE HOUSE in 1872 for favorite son and bride, architecture closely styled to "Das Grosse Haus" built for leader and family earlier. Mansion was stately but offered few comforts. Each of two floors has two large rooms, at end of each a large fireplace, only provision for heating and cooking. Resting on cedar stumps, practically indestructible as foundations, house is solid to this day.

FOUNDER OF COLONY is buried in family plot. Nearby is grave of daughter Aurora for whom village was named.

pathetic believers. Some six thousand acres were acquired, the center of it to be called Bethel, House of God. For a time the colony prospered but then came trouble — antagonism on the part of neighbors, several seasons of bad weather for crops and general discouragement.

By 1855 Keil had acquired the title "Doctor" and many ideas. The real New Jerusalem, he said, must be in the much talked about Oregon Territory and that was where the colony was going. The faithful gathered up their belongings, said farewell to loved ones and prepared to leave.

Also by this time the Doctor had five sons, the eldest named for his father and called Willie. He was nineteen and enthused about the trip west but was suddenly beset by malaria. Before he died he begged his father not to leave him in Missouri but take his body on the caravan and bury it in the new land. Following his promise, Keil placed the boy's body in the sealed casket with the alcohol and placed it on the lead wagon.

After four months of travel the party arrived at

ELIAS KEIL, born in father's house two years after it was built, two years before death of grandfather Keil, lived in structure all his life, never knew electricity or inside plumbing. Picture shows back porch covered by old grapevine.

Willapa, Washington Territory, the originally planned destination, and Willie was buried there. After a short stay, however, Dr. Kiel became dissatisfied with the place as a permanent site for his colony and again pulled up stakes.

Arriving in the Willamette Valley, the Doctor selected a location on the west bank of Mill Creek, just above its junction with the Pudding River and near the Willamette which received the waters of both.

It was share and share alike for everybody except Dr. Keil and many of the names of the colony founders might have come straight out of the Prussian army — Rapp, Steinbock, Wolff, Koch and Koenig. All members were to live by these tenets: "From every man according to his capacity to every man according to his needs, is the rule that runs through the law of love. Every man or woman must be a brother or sister to every man and woman in our family under the law of God."

The autocratic leader set standards of modesty for the homes of colony members yet his own, one of the first to be erected, was three stories tall. It had four very large rooms, two on each floor. There was no central heating system, large fireplaces at each end sufficed for heating and cooking. Two large balconies with railings of turned spindles graced the front of the imposing mansion.

Communal activities were varied and included working in the fine orchards and selling the fruit to neighboring settlers. A large furniture factory was set up, its products sold up and down the valley as were bakery goods. A fine band was organized, playing concerts from the balcony of one large building and for celebrations in neighbor'ng towns. Dr. Keil was quite willing it should be so — for $50, of course. Proceeds of all projects were divided for the benefit of all — or so it was believed by devout members. Some detractors outside the colony claimed the funds went into a stout trunk which reposed under Dr. Keil's four-poster.

However no one in the colony seems to have suffered from want, especially of food. This item seems to have been all important in the progress of Aurora in true old country folk tradition. At all summer celebrations long tables were set up in the open and lavishly spread with German sausages, roasts, pies and pastries — all the rich indigestibles of peasant land. The band played loudly while everyone ate, the record says, and it is assumed the musicians had already eaten.

At Christmas huge baskets of cakes, fruits and candies were distributed to the colonists. Two large fir trees were trussed up in the forty by eighty

church, where the altar was built in the shape of a star. Preaching and band concerts went on almost constantly, gifts accumulated under the trees until New Year's when they were passed out to the children.

Outsiders, even compiete strangers, were welcome at all celebrations and came in droves. It was good business, spreading the good word of Aurora's products. When the railroad came through it stopped for meals at Aurora rather than at Portland which was much larger and only a few miles farther on. Schools operated the year around, allowing no such nonsense as summer vacations. Nor were any educational frivolities tolerated. Reading, writing and arithmetic were the only studies with the exception of music.

Dr. Keil's despotic rule prevailed for twenty-five years, then an undercurrent of change was felt. Many of the original colonists were aging, as was the leader himself. A younger generation was exposed to the outside world and this influence was working its way in. As long as the word of Dr. Keil was undisputed, the colony held together as a unit but he was failing, his word weakening, his grip loosening.

There was a reorganization, a deviation from the credo "Equal service, equal obligation, equal reward," yet still tempered to the older order while Dr. Keil lived. Upon his death in 1877, the colony was dissolved, all communally held property divided between members according to length of service. And as the years passed evidence of the original colony began to disappear, old buildings and houses falling victim to fire and slow decay.

Across the stream, on the highway, a town of Aurora grew up, somewhat as a development of the colony. It was a thriving community for years during the early twentieth century when it was on the main Pacific Highway and a center of the huge hop growing industry of the valley. It had at least one newspaper, the weekly AURORA BOREALIS, starting in 1900 and lasting eight years. Now the Portland-Salem freeway has bypassed the town which retains many reminders of more flourishing times. The community is beginning to realize the importance of its history and is making an effort to preserve its old buildings and visible reminders of its past.

SOUTH END of venerable house shows basement entrance at ground level. Elias Keil, grandson of colony leader, was born here August 17, 1875 and occupied it all his life. He played in famous Aurora Band most of these years, even participating in program at Aurora's Centennial in 1956 at over 80 years of age.

BUTTEVILLE, OREGON

The paddle-wheel steamer SHOALWATER was no more but her bones had been reshaped, her decks relaid, her defects covered with thick white paint. And there was her owner pointing proudly to her new name — FENIX. Funny name, people of the Willamette Valley said. What's it mean? "Why that," explained the owner, "that's the bird in the fable that rose up out of the ashes to fly again. See the point? I know how it should be spelled but this way I could make the letters bigger."

And what had happened to the SHOALWATER? One day in May, 1853, making her landing at the Butteville dock, above the falls where Oregon City is now, the Willamette River swollen by spring rains and flowing savagely, the skipper laid on all the steam she had and called for more. The SHOAL-WATER had the spirit but her flues were weak and a great blast rent the boilers. On deck ready to disembark, the passengers suddenly found themselves in the cold currents. All were in luck to be saved from drowning but none of them ever wanted to hear the name SHOALWATER again.

Etienne Lucier planted the first crop in French Prairie, a flat, treeless area along the Willamette about 1830. The crop was wheat and from then on, until about the turn of the century wheat was almost the only agricultural product of the area — this in a land where the soil was capable of producing anything suitable to a temperate climate. Wheat found a ready market and that was enough. The only real difficulty at first was getting the crop to that market since there were no roads, only the river, and cargoes had to be portaged around large falls and rapids at Oregon City and transferred to

OLD BUTTEVILLE — picture taken from opposite bank of Willamette River about 1890, judging from fact concrete dock has replaced wooden one on pilings. Most buildings shown have vanished but white frame house upper right, ornate one center right and plainer frame with porch extreme left, still remain. Section of deeply rutted road leading to dock gives some idea of difficulties wagons encountered on most roads in western Oregon's rainy season.

ORIGINAL LANDINGS were built on pilings, some remarkably preserved after 100 years or more. Level of river shown here is average. Willamette has become much more tractable in recent years with flood control in main river and such tributaries as Santiam which originates in Cascade Mountains, although even now it goes on rampage when snows melt rapidly or during protracted rainfall.

other craft for the rest of the trip to Fort Vancouver.

All this effort caused a rash of little towns to spring up along the Willamette between the present Salem and Oregon City. Butteville, at the extreme northern end of the wheat belt called French Prairie, was one of these. It was primarily a river landing and never progressed much beyond that although it did boast a church, schools, stores and several saloons during the golden period of wheat shipping.

Joel Palmer, the man who had pioneered a route for the first wagons over the shoulder of Mt. Hood, mentioned the settlement in his journal in 1845; "Eight miles from Pudding River is a village called Butes. It was laid out by Messrs. Abernathy and Beers. There were but a few cabins there when I left. The proprietor had erected a warehouse to store wheat they might purchase of the settlers, who should find it convenient to sell their crops at this point. At this place are some conical hills called

Butes, which arise to considerable heights; the sides and tops of them are covered with tall fir trees which can be seen from the valley for sixty miles." All this was essentially true, the exceptions being one butte of noteworthy height and that only 427 feet, hardly noticeable except locally. His spelling of Bute was common enough in those days.

The village that grew up beside the first crude river landing about 1840 was first called by the preponderately French settlers La Butte but Americanized a few years later. When George Abernathy and Alanson Beers drove pilings at the edge of the river and laid out a simple town, they had big ideas of a metropolis that would outshine the rival Champoeg. For instance they planned to handle the buying and shipping of the settlers — almost to a man retired French Canadian trappers of the Hudson's Bay Co. — and later they would sell real estate, establish stores and saloons. Since there was little or no gold and business was done in trade, the rancher would get his pay in groceries and spend the rest of what he had coming for liquor or wine, Abernathy and Beers making a profit at every turn.

However this was not to come about. Abernathy became involved in the simple politics of the day and was so dedicated to seeing the provisional government get off on the right foot he was elected first governor of Oregon in 1845 and had no time to promote his interests in Butteville. The facts about Beers are obscure but it is known the first real store at the landing was started about 1850 by one Francis Xavier Mathieu, who talked the vacillating Etienne Lucier into casting his vote with the Americans at Champoeg (see Champoeg story).

Mathieu was one of the early French Canadian trappers who with the decline of the fur industry had settled on French Prairie in 1842. He lived with Lucier two years, making himself generally useful as a builder of wagons and houses, then married Rose Osant, daughter of another ex-trapper. Two years later he took a donation claim at La Butte. Mathieu had "a way with people" and after his successful persuasion of the deciding votes in Champoeg, he was elected constable, often settling disputes by inviting contestants to dinner and the difficulty was usually settled amicably over a bottle of French wine.

Mathieu decided against a comparative retirement to run the store. He cut trees on his claim and laid the logs for the lower half of the building and had some whipsawed for the upper section. Handadzed planks served for a floor and split cedar shakes for the roof. From then on for fifteen years Mathieu's Store was the most important place in Butteville. One good customer was Robert Newell of Champoeg, another the Hudson's Bay Co. emissary, Michael Framboise. For two years he had a partner, a George La Roque. A plat of Butteville in the Historical Atlas Map of Marion and Linn Counties, 1878, shows the La Roque claim as entirely surrounding the townsite of Butteville and seems to include it.

In 1860 an Episcopal Church was built, prudently quite high on the bank. Funds for construction came short of a bell but the congregation felt that God, in time, would provide. Next year the big flood that washed through so many river towns inundated Champoeg, wrecked the sister church there and carried its belfry, complete with bell, down to Butteville and depositing it in a thicket along the creek bank. Champoeg, utterly destroyed, had no more use for the bell, so it was joyfully reclaimed, cleaned of mud and hung in the Butteville steeple.

As long as there were few roads, and these almost impassable in wet weather, Butteville flourished. When rumors circulated that the Oregon and California Railroad would stop there, it was hoped farmers would continue to haul wheat in and that it would be shipped by train. But the rails bypassed Butteville and the town gradually faded. Today it is still alive, a tiny and picturesque hamlet with only one business, a modern little grocery store in one of the old, revamped buildings.

LITTLE OLD BUTTEVILLE SCHOOL shown here all prettied up and moved to grounds of Newell home at Champoeg, restored by D.A.R. While exterior of old structure has been renewed, interior is almost unchanged. Original flooring is of whipsawed planks, walls of lighter boards also showing whipsaw marks. School has two rooms, upper and lower grades in former days, is presumed same building as that of "Butteville Academy" incorporated at state legislature in 1869, Francois Xavier Mathieu being one of trustees. Howard McKinley Corning, in his definitive book, **Willamette Landings**, says the Academy "probably was a large name for a small public school." Dolores Purdue, now of Portland, remembers the time she attended graduation exercises at school; "There were three graduates from the 8th grade. After they received their diplomas there was a picnic followed by all kinds of games and races."

IMPRESSIVE MONUMENT in family plot of George La Roque. Smaller stones mark resting places of "Father", "Mother" and other members. Among other La Roque business enterprises was partnership with Mathieu in general store, most important single business in history of Butteville. In 87 years since monument was placed, heavy crop of lichens has become established on stones, encouraged by damp climate.

CHAMPOEG, OREGON

"A ball was given on the floor of Dr. John Mc-Loughlin's mill in Oregon City. Lt. Peel bet the wine with the late Dr. Robert Newell that most of those present would take the British side in case of a contest. Lt. Peel lost the bet and showing some chagrin in his manner, offered to bet another bottle of wine that a man he indicated sitting right opposite to him across the floor would fight under the British flag. Dr. Newell took the bet. The man was asked to cross the floor when the question was put to him. 'Sir, which flag would you support in case of a war for this country?' The answer was quick and clear. 'I fight underneath the Stars and Stripes, myself'. The man was Willard H. Reese."

This incident was related by S. F. Chadwick a number of years later. It gives a vivid glimpse into the way events were building up to trouble with Great Britain over the Oregon country, as to whose flag was to fly over it. "Oregon" at that time was a vast territory extending from Pacific Ocean to Rocky Mountains, between parallels 42 and 54-40. The controversy centered in a rolling, grassy "prairie" area extending from the Indian village of Chemeketa, near where the State Capitol at Salem now stands, northward to a point just south of the Willamette falls at Oregon City. Possibly this land had once been covered by the same dense forests that mantled the surrounding country but native

OLD PICTURE, said to have been taken at Champoeg is undated but scene is typical of early days in busy river town. River is low, exposing bare banks where normal highway would bring it near grass. Phenomenal flood which destroyed Champoeg sent waters high above any point shown here.

"DOCTOR" ROBERT NEWELL, whose title was given for courtesy and affection, was one of earliest and most picturesque of Oregon pioneers. All his buildings and property in Champoeg, except home on higher ground, were washed away in disastrous flood of 1861. Newell persisted in trying to rebuild town for time but became disheartened and moved to Lapwai, Idaho, in middle '60s. Indian friends donated land to him in what became the heart of Lewiston. Portrait here was made on visit to Washington with Indian group to agitate for betterment of their situation.

Indian tribes, loosely grouped as Calapooias, had long been in a habit of setting fire to the grass and brush each fall, to corral game for easy killing and discourage forest growth.

To the earliest settlers in the 1820s the land seemed waiting to be planted to wheat. Etienne Lucier, born in the District of St. Edouard near Montreal, came to this part of the Willamette Valley in those years. He had been a recruited member of the Wilson Price Hunt Expedition overland to Astoria, arriving there in 1812. The arduous trip was part of Astor's great venture to establish a branch of the Pacific Fur Co. at the mouth of the Columbia River. Lucier became a trapper and guide, saw the fertile fields of the Willamette Valley and decided to settle there, planting wheat he brought from the post at Fort Vancouver, Lucier was Oregon's first farmer.

During the '30s more French Canadians gave up trapping, "married" Indian girls, termed "infidel women" by the priests who established missions at nearby St. Louis and St. Paul. Inept at farming to begin with, these "Mountain Men" were soon producing wheat in a golden flood, using it to pay for all manner of food and supplies in place of money.

A system was established to get the grain to market. Many of the farms centered on the banks of the Willamette River at a point called "Encampment du Sable". A landing and warehouse were built there, "batteaux" loaded with grain and floated to the falls at Oregon City where larger boats reloaded the cargo below the falls. Dr. John McLoughlin at Fort Vancouver found a good sale for the crop in Russian settlements along the coast.

Encampment du Sable took on the more convenient name of the Indian village nearby—Champoeg. The origin of the name, according to one version is that it is a combination of two Indian words for "weed" — "champoo" and "coich", pronunciation similar to "shampooik".

By 1840 there were fifty families on the "French Prairie", most of them near Champoeg. At first all were French Canadians with Calapooia or Nez Perce wives and numerous progeny, but later Americans joined the community so that Protestants, particularly Methodists, mingled with the Catholics. There was little friction since in this remote country every man had to rely closely on his neighbor.

Yet there was a storm of vaster implications brewing in high levels — the dispute between the United States and Great Britain as to who would control these fertile lands of the entire Oregon area. On October 28, 1818 a treaty of joint occupancy had been signed in London. In 1827 this was renewed but now more and more American settlers began to chafe at the idea of a possible English government. When the discontent finally reached an explosive stage, it was less a quarrel than the need to settle a private estate amicably.

Ewing Young, who became one of the wealthiest settlers, died in 1841 without an heir, his lands, buildings and stocks unclaimed. Now in place of the social and religious meetings the settlers were accustomed to have, they gathered to appoint an executor. At the same time another kind of meeting was called to cope with losses of livestock from wolves and other predatory animals, specifically losses of cattle and horses running wild on the Young place after his death.

On February 2, 1843 the farmers met again and levied an assessment of five dollars on each to pay bounty for carcasses of marauding wolves, mountain lions, lynx or bear. It was aptly termed a "Wolf Meeting" and the phrase applied to others following. A second Wolf Meeting was held on March 2 but this time wolves were not discussed.

The Americans, now about equal in number to those of foreign origin, were in some ferment over fear of British control and it was agreed by all that a local government of some kind must be established. A committee of twelve was appointed to "take into consideration the propriety for taking measures for civil and military protection of this colony." The committee met at Willamette Falls within a few days and arranged for a general gathering at Champoeg on May 2 to vote on the situation.

That meeting was the most momentous and dramatic in the history of the Oregon country, resulting in a bloodless decision that the vast territory should be under the control of the United States rather than Great Britain.

It was called to order in a corner of the wheat warehouse, used as an office by the Hudson's Bay Co. The first resolutions, calling for organization into a self-governing body, generated such excitement and confusion in the confined quarters that many voters went unheard and many of those who did hear voted improperly, even for the opposing side. The whole gathering then moved outdoors to the middle of a field and while the situation was

NEWELL HOME about turn of century, prudently built on high ground above Champoeg. House fell rapidly into disrepair after abandonment and when it collapsed, D.A.R. made project of restoring it. Present house on site is relic-filled museum, containing some original boards and fireplace bricks, is maintained as historical shrine.

OLD CHAMPOEG CEMETERY was on ground too high for flood-waters. Section shown here was planted with lilacs, now gnarled, lichen-encrusted, but still blooming in spring. Contrary to fate of some old cemeteries, this one is maintained for historical significance.

improved, a voice vote was hopeless. Trapper Joe Meek, tall, dark-eyed and black-bearded, raised his penetrating voice against the uproar, urging the men to "side up" in the field and declaring he would start things by taking the American side. French Canadian G. W. LeBriton made the formal motion that this be done and it was seconded by American William Gray, a Methodist mission worker. Joe Meek stepped out and called on all those of the one hundred and two present who wanted an American government established to gather around him.

With a loud hallooing forty-nine men went to the American side to make fifty in all. And fifty remained where they were. The other two? They were Etienne Lucier and F. X. Mathieu, standing in the middle, hesitating. Everyone waited impatiently for them to make up their minds. Lucier said he had

heard that under American rule, the very windows of his house would be taxed. Mathieu, who owned much land and property in nearby Butteville where he was surrounded by American sympathizers, suddenly decided to go with them and persuaded Lucier to do the same. They joined Meek and swayed the vote. The immense area sandwiched between Mexican California and Canada, so tenuously held by England, was now safely under the flag of the United States — at least as far as the inhabitants were concerned. Succeeding events soon made it official.

A group of nine was named to set up the beginnings of the infant government and a short time later Champoeg was declared "The Capital." A crude State House was erected of split cedar slabs and poles, roofed with cedar bark.

England was not willing to go along with all this quite so easily and in 1844 was still contending with Washington although it had ceased any activities in the Oregon country, the issue seeming dangerous to everybody but the Oregonians. There was even talk of war but the increasing influx of American immigrants to the Willamette Valley over the Oregon Trail made it obvious to the British that their cause was lost.

Champoeg began to take on the appearance of a permanent town, largely through the efforts of Robert Newell. Two places in Ohio, Putnam and Zanesville, are mentioned as his birthplace, in 1807. At eighteen he became a Rocky Mountain trapper, then as the fur trade declined, he teamed up with Joe Meek on a trip to the Oregon country, spending some time in Idaho and acquiring Nez Perce wives. They were sisters, daughters of sub-chief Kow-e-so-te. With a third man they brought the first wagons from Fort Hill into Oregon, although half dismantled. When they stopped at the mission in Walla Walla, Marcus Whitman congratulated the young men, saying: "You will never regret your efforts. Now that you have brought the first wagons, others will follow."

Newell, often referred to as "Doctor" or more familiarly as "Doc", took up residence in Champoeg and began to raise a family. He bought and fitted up two batteaux, starting a regular run between the town and the falls above Oregon City. They were called MOGUL and BEN FRANKLIN, power provided by Indian paddlers.

By 1851, when steamboats reached the town, Newell abandoned his primitive vessels and turned to real estate. Having taken up the 360-acre claim of Walter Pomeroy at the southern edges of Champoeg, he laid out a sub-division and sold lots. When need for land access became acute, he persuaded the provisional legislature to survey and construct a stage road from Salem to his property which he called Oxford. The Salem-St. Paul-Champoeg road is essentially the same route today.

By the 1850s there were about a hundred and fifty buildings in Champoeg including adjoining Oxford where Newell had built a fine home on a higher level above the Willamette. Peter Skene Ogden and James Douglas reported in 1847 that the Hudson's Bay Co. property in Champoeg was worth about $8,500 and the concern sold out in 1852 for some $17,000. Values and building continued to increase until the catastrophe of 1861 which all but wiped out the progressing city.

The Willamette had risen in 1853-54 to the point where water flowed through the edges of Champoeg and nibbled at the foundations of buildings. The stream subsided with little damage but Champoeg citizens were not alert to the warning.

In 1861, September and October passed with almost no precipitation. Then it began to rain in earnest and November brought an unending deluge which turned to snow. Temperatures rose, rain continued and the snowbanks melted.

Every tributary of the main stream, particularly the raging Santiam, swelled the Willamette almost a foot an hour until by December 2 the river was fifty-five feet higher than summer stage and twelve feet above the level of the '53-'54 flood. This time the murky, roaring waters swept over the town seven feet deep with terrific force, large logs acting as battering rams, and one by one Champoeg's buildings were carried away. The river stayed up for several days then slowly subsided to reveal a townsite "bare as a sandy beach". Three hundred and fifty houses were washed downstream yet the destruction was not quite total. Two solidly constructed structures remained standing — the two saloons.

The higher bench where Robert Newell had his house remained dry, the house intact. Newell, however, was financially ruined, his holdings in town entirely swept away. His Indian wife had died long before and now he took his new white wife and many offsprings to Lewiston, Idaho, the scene of his youthful dalliance.

Attempts were made to lay out a new town on the old site but with its moving spirit gone, once so strong many people thought of the place as Newellsville, nothing much happened. The green

meadow where the fateful vote was taken is now marked by a granite shaft, its exact location determined in 1900 by the last surviving voter, Francois Xavier Mathieu. It is emblazoned with the names believed on best authority to be of those siding with Meek and the United States. Surrounding all is Champoeg State Park where thousands hold summer picnics. The author visits there often, one such occasion in November when heavy rain was making a lake of the picnic grounds, tables and benches floating. The Willamette will continue periodic rampages; present and future dams along the tributaries such as the Detroit and Santiam appreciably restraining flood levels.

UNIQUE MONUMENT in Champoeg burial ground shows full maiden name of wife in accordance with Catholic custom. Object is partly to maintain evidence of accuracy of birth, baptismal records. English ivy, established and growing wild in much of Willamette Valley, clambers around base of marker. At least one marker in cemetery dates back to 1853. It is thought longvanished wooden ones were first placed by settlers in '30s.

OLD FARM HOUSE built by Zorn family in early days is still occupied by descendants. Bell in steeple was used to call men from fields for meals and emergencies.

BUENA VISTA, OREGON

The lone shack near the river was the only habitation in miles and no doubt Reason B. Hall thought whoever lived there would be glad to see a stranger. Probably he was — but for a special reason. He answered Hall's knock, said his name was Heck but very little more. Later he told Hall he had an urgent business matter to attend to and could Hall stay at the little two-room cabin to watch out for vandals or Indians until he got back? Hall said he could and moved in, carrying everything he owned. The stay stretched out for days, weeks and months. After a year and no Heck, Hall figured no man ever got a cabin any easier.

The place was on the west bank of the Willamette River where the first industrial city of Oregon would be built. Reason Hall was a veteran of the War of 1812 and the Black Hawk affray of 1834. He arrived in Oregon in 1846, at Heck's shanty a year later and was laying out a city on the site about 1853. He hired a surveyor named Medows (locally referred to as Meaders) Vanderpool to line the streets and lots. New towns of the day were often named for patriotic reasons, such as Independence and Lincoln, and following the trend Hall named his Liberty. Later Buena Vista seemed more appropriate since several of his kinsmen had fought in the Mexican War battle of Buena Vista. Hall may not have understood the Spanish significance of the name but the site did offer a "beautiful view", any of several gentle rises affording splendid panoramas of the fertile Willamette Valley and its curving river.

Even before Hall's town was platted it had a general store, started in 1851 by partners Weil and Sharf who soon added a warehouse. As travelers arrived some complained because, while their destination was Rocky Point, Judkin's Landing or Sidney's Landing, all on the west side of the river, they had no way to get across except by rowboat, swimming their horses and who wanted to remount a wet horse? So Hall started a ferry in '52, beginning what is one of the longest, continuously operating ferry services — allowing for occasional breakdowns and layups by floods — in Oregon. Even today, 114 years later, the traveler still crosses the river at this point by ferry.

Other businesses were established rapidly. James A. O'Neal decided his town of Wheatland, wheat shipping point thirty miles down river, would soon take second place to the new metropolis and moved to Buena Vista, starting the second general store. The inevitable grist mill in this land of rolling wheat fields was built about the same time. H. D. Godley put up a hotel, and one of Reason Hall's sons, E. C., opened a wagon shop where the forge glowed red almost constantly. Reason's daughter Mary married Henry Croisant who came to Buena Vista after a short and disillusioning stay in the gold fields of California. A number of descendants of this union still live in Salem, Oregon, twenty-one miles distant. One, George William Croisant, has an insurance business there.

In 1856 Oregon was anticipating entry into the union as a state. Centers of population were in the shipping ports and infant industrial towns along the Willamette River. Competition among these for the juicy prize of state capitol was intense. No shy violet, Reason Hall saw his embryo town of Buena Vista as out in front but felt he could urge it on even more by judicious publicity. He made a trip to Oregon City and inserted an ad in the OREGON SPECTATOR April 21, 1856 — flamboyant but adhering strictly to the truth. One paragraph stated: "The ground is dry, and ascending the river bank, a more healthful situation cannot be found in the country—no swamp or low or wet land about the place, and is backed by as beautiful and as rich country as there is in Oregon." As an added incentive, Hall wrote: "There are plenty of the best building timbers handy to the place and thousands of cords of cordwood". He made the generous offer "to the people of Oregon as much ground as will be wanted to set the State House on, also available as fine a stone quarry as any I have seen in Oregon." Reason's spelling at the end failed to equal his enthusiasm. "There is a good steamboat landing on the Wallamet river. Come forward and pole your votes for Buena Vista." But the little river community hardly made a showing in the voting, Salem taking first place.

Yet the town went ahead. By now many river boats which before ended their runs at downstream landings, were including Buena Vista. A school was started in a one-room log house in 1859 which served as church on Sundays. And three years later a post office was established. But while hotels, saloons, schools, stores and blacksmith shops were all part of the economy, the town's real growth and fame came from an industry unique in Oregon, a stoneware and pottery plant.

When Freeman Smith's six sons were mustered out of the Union Army at the end of the Civil War, they joined him with the mother and four daughters in migrating to the Far West via the Isthmus of Panama. Arriving in Oregon in late 1865, the father heard about a deposit of clay on the banks of the Willamette at Buena Vista which had excellent firing qualities. Freeman Smith, who had worked in an eastern pottery plant, tested the clay in a makeshift kiln and bought clay land on the riverbank near the ferryslip. Then he and his sons went to work building the kilns. A deposit of finer clay needed for glazing, was found at Corvallis, 17 miles away.

Smith and Co. products were eagerly snapped up by local consumers but this small market was soon saturated. Freeman loaded a wagon with his jugs and pots and drove to Albany, confident he would meet with the same ready sale as at home. After a day of discouraging rebuffs and doubts, he was about ready to drive home when he stopped at John Connor's Hardware store. Connor was no more enthusiastic than others but did offer to take the lot on commission, at the rate of 50 cents per gallon capacity. When the potter returned to Albany Smith found the entire stock of 300 gallon capacity sold, Connor paying him in gold.

By 1870 Freeman Smith was ready to retire and sold his interest to son Amendee, who with his brothers, greatly expanded the business, adding such lines as flower pots and sewer pipe. The 15-inch sewer pipeline running down Portland's S.E. Stark Street was manufactured at Buena Vista. At this time the plant was employing four "turners" at the potters' wheels and a crew of ten Chinese for mixing clay.

The town boomed with the pottery business, enough to support two physicians, Drs. J. C. Woods and W. C. Lee, and Woods with a man named March opened a drug store. Buena Vista's

most imposing saloon, owned by John Wade whose specialty was a potent spirit called "Blue Ruin", was sold to Charles Henry. The new owner added several other lines of liquor and an "annex" for the entertainment of lonely traveling men.

The town had its share of fires, the most disastrous one destroying the two-story Wells Store with I.O.O.F. and Knights Templar quarters upstairs. At midnight of Saturday, February 10, 1870 members of the night crew at the pottery plant noticed flames shooting from the frame building. Responding volunteer firemen were barely able to save half the goods from the adjoining Pitkin establishment and were forced to stand by as flames leveled both structures. The fire seemed to have started in the fraternal hall where there had been a dance that evening. Total loss was about $5,000, a serious setback in those times.

Spared by the fire was the notorious "Bust Head" Saloon not far away. This little false-fronted drink emporium from which the more troublesome drunks were ejected out the back door into a gulch, was the incubator for most of Buena Vista's crime. One sensational act of violence in the little river town was perpetrated by one Tubbs, accustomed to nurse his grievances at the saloon. Oregon historian Ben Maxwell tells the story.

Tubbs, with an extensive criminal record, was so abusive to his wife that although pregnant, she left him, taking refuge with relatives, the George Geer family. On a hot Fourth of July in 1878, Tubbs passed Beech's Drug Store. Beech was sitting in front although most merchants had closed up and joined a citizen's march to Independence to celebrate the holiday. In a friendly tone he remarked to Tubbs: "Sure is a hot day, isn't it?" Tubbs was reported to have answered in a "surly fashion": "Yes it is, and it will be a day long remembered in Buena Vista." It was.

About 2 P.M., B. F. Hall, son of Reason, was sitting on his front porch when he heard several shots coming from the Geer home. He hurried over and was just in time to see Mrs. Tubbs reel from the front door and collapse under a big oak tree. While other neighbors tried to help the wounded woman, he rushed in the house and found Tubbs on the floor bleeding profusely from gun shot wounds. He picked up the gun near Tubbs' hand and saw all chambers of the old style five-shooter had been discharged. Several other men came in and the report states: "The men wore sneers on their faces as they watched Tubbs die." The wife soon expired also

ODD FELLOWS' HALL was built in 1870s, replacing older srtucture, destroyed by fire. Two stories tall, building is now boarded up.

GNARLED, MOSS-DAPPLED LIMBS of old oak form strong pattern against early spring sky. Called "Oregon", this oak **Quercus Garryana**, ranged from Vancouver Island through California's coastal mountains. This specimen stands at edge of Buena Vista street, once spread branches over long-gone home of George Geer, and under it the murdered Mrs. Tubbs died.

and all agreed it was a plain case of murder and suicide.

In this kind of weather prompt attention had to be given to burial arrangements so several villagers made coffins, the next day B. F. Hall loading them on his wagon and driving to the cemetery on the hill. Mrs. Tubbs was interred there but her husband-murderer was buried unceremoniously in adjacent, scrubby land. Sometime later Hall observed the soil had been disturbed and a little digging revealed an empty space. Discreet inquiry disclosed the fact that two Polk County doctors paid a "resurrection man" $50 to remove Tubbs' remains, clean and sack them, row the gruesome cargo down river to Independence on a moonless night.

At its height Buena Vista was one of the most important places along the Willamette and population warranted a large, two-story school. The pottery plant was easily the most important industry, employing several hundred men and second in size was a busy sawmill. Hops were introduced by Adam Weiser in 1867 and became a main crop almost immediately, holding top place for 70 years. But as the years went by many factors gradually killed this prosperity, the worst blow being the bypassing, by several miles, of the railroad. Hops declined in demand and value and the pottery plant moved to the larger Portland market. Salem, as capitol, drew away most of the population.

Today the town is quiet and almost all the buildings are gone, including the houses, their locations indicated in spring by shoals of yellow daffodils. The Smith Market still operates, the only one that does. The cemetery on the hill is well cared for, commanding an impressive view for miles of the Willamette and lush farm lands. Many markers are of marble, some beautifully sculptured. An open area would seem to indicate graves once marked with wooden headboards which decayed early in the moist climate. Mrs. Tubbs' grave would likely be one of them and orchards have long since concealed any trace of her slayer's violated resting place.

CLASPED HANDS, sculptured in marble, were favorite symbol for headstone decorations in early days. This well preserved example adorns marker of Reason Hall and immediate family. Hall was first permanent settler of Buena Vista and founder of town. He died Dec. 12, 1869 at 76, was buried at left of stone, his wife who outlived him by several years, at right. Old cemetery contains remains of sixty descendants of Reason Hall.

ORTLEY, OREGON

The Cascade Mountain range, extending in a north and south direction through Washington and Oregon, exerts a very strong climatic effect on the western and eastern sections of both states. The barrier causes most marine storms common to the area to deposit most of their moisture on the westerly slope and holds back much of the colder air prevailing in winter on the eastern side. But there is a rift in this wall, the gorge cut through the Cascades by the Columbia River. Terrific winds whistle through the gorge much of the time at some seasons, their direction depending upon the location of high and low pressure areas. Strangely enough, this geographical peculiarity had a direct effect in making a ghost of a thriving, growing town.

On an exposed plateau on the eastern side of the summit of the Cascades high above the Columbia huddle the few remnants of Ortley, once bustling with 300 people dedicated to the dream of making a fortune growing Ortley apples.

About 1908, a group of business men in Hood River, Oregon, began to work on the idea of establishing a European type of community for the purpose of establishing a large orchard of apples and of creating a world-wide market for them. They selected comparatively level fields on a bluff surmounting high cliffs facing the Columbia — a spectacular setting offering a view of many miles up and down the river and of several snow-clad mountain peaks.

In 1911 the plat was filed in Wasco County for the Town of Ortley by the Hood River Orchard and Land Co. Business buildings were to be centralized near the only source of water, a small stream. Close to these stores were to be the residences of the settlers, who would have to radiate out some little distance to their orchards, which would surround the whole. Lots for homes were an acre in size, orchard space was laid out in 5 and 10 acre plots.

As soon as building was begun the need for expert carpenters and other artisans became apparent and ads were inserted in the Portland newspapers.

A Mr. Hallyburton was one carpenter who responded, his skill so evident he was put in charge of the whole building operation. A school was erected, several stores, a fancy two-story hotel elegantly fitted with bath both upstairs and down, and a saloon. In the rear was a huge barn capable of sheltering 200 horses for working the land.

People moved in eager to set out their little apple trees. Early arrivals had to go down the steep mountainside to Mosier, 7 miles away, for mail but on April 9, 1912, the post office was opened with L. D. Firebaugh as first postmaster. As soon as the new Ortley Hotel was completed the post office was moved into the lobby. The hotel also housed a fine dance hall and Saturday nights people came from Mosier, The Dalles and surrounding farms to relax in a big way.

Kerosene lamps provided the only illumination at first but the developers invited the power company in The Dalles to come up and see what was going on. Duly impressed the purveyors of power invested $10,000 in the up and coming community which soon had electric lights.

A garage was built near the hotel to house two elegant new automobiles, a Franklin and a Cadillac. Prospective settlers were met at the train in style and carried up the twisting mountain road to the town on the heights. Here they were put up at the hotel, wined, dined and importuned to buy an apple orchard. And buy they did until young trees

NATIVE TREES on high windswept plateau are hardy pines, firs and oaks, well adapted to fend for selves. Oaks were left around barns and buildings for shade, removed in areas where apple trees were to be grown.

LITTLE SCHOOL HOUSE stands almost intact but long ago converted to shelter for farm machinery. Water stands in road in foreground. Snowy Cascades show in distance.

flanked the whole countryside. By this time the land company had sunk $200,000 in the project, and had the settlers paid cash for their property, it would at least have broken even. But they had not paid even a fraction of what they owed.

Then some painful truths began to appear. Many apple trees died from lack of water in summer, drowning in an excess of it in winter, there being little or no drainage. And the trees that lived were having their troubles. There were many large

fir trees along the bluffs with branches on only one side due to the strong prevailing winds blowing up the river in the growing season. So eager were the settlers to cultivate their ground and get their trees started, they did not question the reason for the lopsided firs until the apple trees began to be distorted the same way.

This discouraging state of affairs caused the orchardists who had bought on contract to quit and move away. Before long the population had dwin-

71

HOUSES AND BUILDINGS not razed or salvaged for lumber soon disintegrated among native trees which formed grove around nucleus of town. Soil is almost impermeable, rains of winter stand as surface ground water. In summer ground dries into something resembling adobe bricks, cracking and killing roots of susceptible apple trees.

dled to a low point and the post office was closed in November, 1922. Ortley was getting to be a very lonely place for Mr. Hallyburton, the builder, who had decided to hang on, no matter what. And remain he did until he was the sole resident.

The power company was anxious to take its poles and lines down, salvaging what it could from the fiasco but old Hallyburton paid his electric service bill of $1.10 per month regularly and promptly and all the company could do was sit on its hands, hoping for a slip up in the payments. The Community Hall, hotel and other buildings were torn down and the old man held on tenaciously until 1946. Then even he abandoned the place, the light poles and most of the apple trees still living pulled up and desolation in Ortley was complete.

MARYHILL, WASHINGTON

In its journey to the sea the Columbia River makes its final turn west through timbered mountains and then a desert of barren rocks and cliffs. No spectacle could be more astonishing than the immense gray castle sprawling high on one of the river's bordering palisades.

The pile is best viewed from across the river on the Oregon side. The observing traveler up the Columbia gorge may well ask: "What, for goodness sakes — is that?" That, the traveler's guide will usually say, is Maryhill Castle. "It was built by Sam Hill, son of the railroad tycoon, Jim Hill, as a monument to his mother." However, Samuel was not the son of the "Empire Builder", James Hill, but his son-in-law. He was a trusted employee of Jim Hill at first, then in 1888 married the oldest daughter of his boss — Mary Hill. Jim did have a son Louis, but the brothers-in-law were not overly compatible. The unanswered questions are — did Sam Hill build the castle as a memorial for his wife, as a palace-residence, or did he foresee its ultimate use as a museum?

Samuel Hill majored in law at Harvard and was admitted to the bar in 1880. Jim Hill engaged young Sam to help him fight some legal battles, then admitted him to his giant railroad combine, allowing him to carry on his own legal practice and make some profitable investments. He traveled extensively, making friends in high places everywhere. One of these was Queen Marie of Roumania, who would later dedicate his castle on the cliffs.

Samuel Hill was personable, shrewd and eccentric. Shortly before the end of World War I, he bought some 7,000 acres of rock and sagebrush which surprised no one who knew him but did intrigue them. When Sam announced he was going to set up a colony for Quakers from Belgium, he raised more questions than he answered. Was the project a purely benevolent gesture or was he planning to add more millions to his coffers with cheap foreign labor?

The ground planned for the colony on the Washington side of the Columbia was opposite Biggs Junction in Oregon. The site included a long established village called Columbus, an agricultural center, the gently sloping ground on the river's shore deep and fertile — a bench extending about half a mile to suddenly rising cliffs of barren rock and scanty soil only a little less arable. A wagon road wound up a steep gully to the summit and along this the colonists would be quartered in cottages Hill would build. On both sides of the steeply sloping valley rose vertical cliffs, partly separated into palisades, each surmounted by a rounded dome of rocks, soil and sand. On the top of the highest one, Samuel Hill, in 1913, started construction of what would be the most conspicuous structure anywhere along the Columbia, an imposing feudal-type castle, such as those that stand along the Rhine.

LITTLE CHURCH was serving community of Columbus when Samuel Hill appeared, turned town into supply center for building of Maryhill Castle, changing name of town to Maryhill. Tycoon kept church in good condition during "occupation" but it has deteriorated. Building is set on low bench of river bank, grass and trees showing fertility of narrow band of soil, barren hills making up background.

SIMULATED STONEHENGE—one of Sam Hill's projects in connection with castle—"exact" replica of mysterious place of ancient worship or astronomy near Salisbury, England. In original only few of pillars retain connecting slabs, only two of original five gigantic trilithons surrounding central altar or sacrificial stone. Hill sent engineer, astronomer, other workmen to England to measure and make plaster casts of original rocks, bringing back molds for duplicating them. Hill's interest in Stonehenge stemmed from visit to original where guide informed him flat rock in center was used for human sacrifice. As a Quaker, he was particularly impressed, comparing such useless slaughter of human life to that of war. It was then he conceived idea of erecting similar structure as memorial to war dead. Legend on horizontal slab in center reads: "In memory of Soldiers and Sailors of Klickitat County who gave their lives in defense of their Country. This monument is erected in the hope that others inspired by the example of their valor and their heroism may share in that love of liberty and burn with that fire of Patriotism which death alone can quench."

During the next several years parcels of Quakers came from Belgium and other European countries to look at the rocky ground, searingly hot in summer, swept by icy winds in winter — looked briefly and went away. A scant few did settle for a while, making some effort to coax a crop from the stark land, but they also departed.

While the Samuel Hills lived in a stately mansion in Seattle, construction of the castle went on regardless of the failure of the colonization plans. It was known almost from the start that it would be called Maryhill. Was it named for the wife, Mary Hill? One point seems a fact — although Mary never saw the pile at any time, even from a distance, gossip had it she was a resident, almost a prisoner, a woman with a failing mind.

While the exact purpose of the vast building was never known, possibly even to Sam Hill, it was almost completed by 1926 and in the fall of that year came Queen Marie to dedicate Maryhill Castle. Before leaving Portland for the ceremony, the Queen attended the International Livestock Exposition, sitting with her royal party in a special box. The group made a worthy subject for the newsreels and the royal lady was not above making pin money by endorsing beauty products.

And at Maryhill she found ready a platform erected in front of the gaunt, gray shell. From it one could look east up the Columbia, south into the gorge and down many miles of the river's westerly flow. After the outdoor ceremony everyone hurried indoors for more convivial celebration, then departed to allow workmen to continue plastering walls.

Construction went on a few more years and when completed the interior included electricity,

SAM HILL'S CASTLE dedicated by Queen Marie of Roumania on a dreary, gray early winter day as indicated here. This is conventional rear of structure, more ornate facade commanding almost limitless view of Columbia gorge, shown dimly in background.

plumbing and other refinements foreign to the traditional castle. Samuel Hill died February 6, 1931 in Portland, his ashes taken to Maryhill and deposited in a tomb on the rocky cliff. It was supposed he had not made up his mind to what use the castle would be put, yet in his will he left a handsome endowment in the hands of trustees of the state to perpetuate the building as a museum.

In 1940 Maryhill Museum was opened to the public. It attracts an increasing number of visitors each summer, offering extensive and varied exhibits of painting, sculpture and Indian artifacts. The Throne Room is displayed, complete with furniture including the royal throne itself, all transported from the now vanished Kingdom of Roumania.

PEASANT SHELTER at Maryhill. It was Samuel Hill's wish that the countryside surrounding his feudal castle be filled by Belgian Quaker immigrants. Many did come, a few remained to eke out miserable existence on stony, dry soil of hillsides. Then even these were forced to go elsewhere. Land affords few near-level spots, bluffs in background descending to Columbia River in giant stair steps.

LANDUSKY, MONTANA

From time immemorial Indians in the Little Rockies knew of gold there but it was just some metal too soft to use for tools. Only when the white man showed such eagerness to get his hands on even small bits of it did they pay much attention to the yellow "treasure".

On Thanksgiving Day of 1868, at Fort Browning on the Milk River, the officers' dinner was interrupted by an Indian wanting to see Major Simmons — one Nepee, a familiar figure around the fort. He displayed a pouch filled with gold nuggets and said it was a present to his friend, Major Simmons. Greatly excited, the officers made vigorous attempts to get Nepee to tell where he got the gold but he kept the secret under all promises and threats. If he told it, he said, his people would kill him.

Nepee had a friend, Joe Hontus, with whom he had been camping several summers. Shortly after the incident at the fort Joe got drunk and bragged: "I know where that gold is and I'm going after it." He never returned from the hills, his body was found full of bullet holes along the trail. Nepee died with his secret in 1876.

Powell Landusky arrived in the diggings of Last Chance Gulch as a gangling teenager. Even then he had an ungovernable temper and flew into blind rages. He was joshed about his loose build, his Missouri drawl and one day someone asked him in an imitation of his accent: "Where you from anyhow?" Landusky's reply was a powerful punch that laid the heckler low followed by: "From Pike County, Missouri, by God!" With more respect the people called him Pike.

The man from Missouri was a sworn enemy of any and all Sioux and fell into many encounters with them. In 1880, he and Joe Hamilton were attempting to do some trading with a party of Piegans at a fort the whites had built on Flatwillow Creek. There was trouble, Landusky claiming one of the braves had attacked him with a chunk of wood and tried to stab him in the back. The other Indians were aroused and the two whites fled to the fort kitchen. The window was so small Landusky could just squeeze his head and one arm out to fire at the Indians who were now circling around hurling taunts at the holed-up whites.

The young Piegan Landusky had accused of treachery was hiding behind a bush and now saw the white man's head made a good target, shooting him in the jaw. Landusky jumped back into the room, reloaded his Winchester and started shooting again, this time hitting and killing a squaw. Withdrawing to reload again, an Indian bullet hit him in the body. Staggering with pain and loss of blood from two wounds, Pike clutched at the table edge and before falling, broke off the shattered section of jaw with four teeth in it, still raging as he threw it into the corner. This time he gave up and fell fainting on the bed. The other whites at the besieged fort sent a scout to try to get through to Fort Maginnis for help including a doctor. Scout Healy managed to get through and alerted the army to the situation.

A party of soldiers came with an army doctor who dressed Landusky's wounds and set his broken jaw. The patient lay for days without improvement, raving in delirium most of the time, swallowing whiskey during his lucid moments. His partners knew something drastic would have to be done to save Pike and this was to take him to Lewiston. They made the arduous journey in a week and there

RIGORS OF 70 MONTANA WINTERS have nearly effaced lettering on monument to Powell Landusky whose violent life was ended by bullet from Kid Curry's gun. "Pike" was buried on hill above his ranch, several unidentified graves flanking enclosure.

Dr. DePalme told Landusky the jaw had been badly set, would have to be rebroken and reset. "Break it!" roared Landusky. "If I die, I die!" The doctor performed the operation and the jaw began to heal. Landusky recovered although his face was badly disfigured.

In the spring of 1881, he and his partner went to the newly-booming camp of Maiden in the Judith Mountains and started a saloon. He met a widow, a Mrs. Descry, and in spite of his contorted face, Pike Landusky successfully courted and married her. Justice of the Peace "Pony" McPartland performed the ceremony, the first of its kind in camp. Witnesses were the seven Descry children and most of the local population. In 1884 the Landuskys moved to a beautiful valley just where Rock Creek emerges from the south edge of the Little Rockies.

That same year "Dutch Louie" Myers found some color in nearby Alder Gulch. He had just started work on his claim June 15 when he was joined by Frank Aldrich and Charles Brown prospecting up the same gulch. They decided on a partnership, later inviting Landusky in and Aldrich was sent to Fort Assiniboine for supplies. When he returned in two weeks he found the others had panned gold dust worth $109. With food and supplies they now set to work building sluices and each man was soon cleaning up $20 a day.

At this point Maiden was crowded with prospectors arriving too late to "get in on" the best diggings and when they heard of the strikes at Alder Gulch most of them left for the new bonanza. Among them was "Nigger Eli" Shelby and it was he who found the heaviest deposits of gold on a rim high above the gulch, William Shelton finding the largest nugget, worth $83.

During the lull following the first rush, a seventeen-year old boy named George A. Ottowa joined up with a man named Curtis for a prospecting trip in the surrounding gulches. They located a claim, agreeing that one would dig while the other stood guard. The boy stood the first watch and later he was to write: "I stood guard while Curtis shoveled. Shortly after this I saw Pike Landusky coming down the trail, his big .45 six-shooter strapped to his waist. I drew a bead on him and told him to throw up his hands, which he did, as he had not seen us. He said he wanted to talk to us and I told him to unbuckle his six-shooter and throw it on the trail. He did and came over to where we were standing. He said we could keep our ground."

The men figured there must be some good reason for Landusky's unusually agreeable behavior and there was. He and Dutch Louie had just discovered

DETAILED STUDY of old farm building shows nearly regular marks of broad axe used by pioneer carpenter to dress logs used in construction. Simple mud was used first as chinking, later mortar. Montana is full of historic log buildings, most of round, undressed logs. Good examples of dressed log construction, with flattened sides, are frequently seen in Little Rockies mining camps.

a pocket of nuggets upstream — that was to yield them $5,000 very quickly.

The discoveries of these four men started a bigger stampede than the first but there were complications similar to those in the Black Hills of South Dakota. The new diggings were located on Fort Belknap Indian Reservation and white men were barred from mining, even entering. When news of the strikes reached the Government a detachment of soldiers was sent from Fort Maginnis to a point on the south bank of the Missouri where the miners had established headquarters. Periodically the military would make a raid on the trespassers, lecturing them and ordering them to vacate the reservation. The gold seekers complied but returned when the soldiers left. After several repetitions of these bloodless and fruitless maneuvers, the miners were allowed to stay as long as they brought in no liquor. This order was obeyed with tongue-in-cheek agreement, but the army had done its part.

The start of the big rush that would make the towns of Landusky, Zortman and Ruby Gulch boom began by accident. In August of 1893, Landusky and Robert Orman were prospecting along a ridge, expecting to work it to the end. In mid-afternoon of the hot day they dropped down to the stream for a drink. While scrambling up, a hand broke off a chunk of rich ore. On being crushed and washed the rock yielded a "string of gold three inches long in the pan."

Not being sure their claim was on or off the Belknap Reservation, the pair removed their ore at

SEVERAL ORIGINAL BUILDINGS remain in Landusky, most fast approaching ruin. This one is identified by various residents as "first post office," "general store," seems beyond repair but plans are afoot to restore it.

night. This first discovery, rich as it was, turned out to be a "minor miracle" in light of a later one — a vein thirteen feet wide yielding $500 a ton, the ore free milling, gold easily separated by crushing and washing. And that was only the beginning. Soon ore was yielding them as much as $13,000 a ton. When the rumor that they had obtained $100,000 from a single small hole reached the outside world, the biggest and last stampede was on.

By the middle of next year, 1894, the newspapers of Havre, Helena and Anaconda carried many columns about the big strike and were advocating Landusky as the site for the capitol with such flourishes as: "Hurrah for Landusky for Capitol! Helena and Anaconda are not in it" . . . . . "The boys have enough to pay the national debt after making themselves rich . . . all we need is a stamp to make ourselves $20 gold pieces."

The loosely knit camp called Landusky became

the town of Landusky June 9 when a meeting was held and T. J. Throop appointed recorder. Every "bona fide citizen" was allowed two lots, 50 x 100 feet, providing he erect a building 16 x 18 feet with 10 foot ceiling within 90 days. The Havre ADVERTISER issue containing this news had another item about a development that would have a bearing on events leading to Landusky's end. "Jake Harris, better known as 'Jew Jake', is about to embark in the saloon business." It would be in this saloon that Pike Landusky would meet Kid Curry for the last time.

The magnet that drew the Currys to Landusky was not gold but reports of rich, well watered land at the edge of the Little Rockies. The Curry boys had come here as adept ranch hands, having worked for the Circle Bar and Fergus Land and Cattle Co. At the Little Rockies site the Curry brothers took up a homestead at the mouth of Rock Creek and found themselves neighbors of Pike Landusky whose home was just above beside the spring, a mile and a half below the town of Landusky.

Before arriving the brothers had been known as Logan, the reason for the change to Curry unexplained. Henry, the oldest by several years, was not well and after a short time on the homestead went to Steamboat Springs on the Colorado River for a "cure" but died there. Next youngest was Harvey, better known to history as "The Kid" or "Kid Curry". The next was Johnny, the handsome one and then Loney, handy with women and the fiddle.

The boys were friendly with their notorious neighbors for nine years. The first evidence of bad feeling seems to have come when Pike returned a plow he had borrowed. It was broken, Landusky claiming it was in that condition when he got it, the Currys denying it. The feud gained impetus when Landusky discovered lady-killer Loney was ardently pursuing one of his four step-daughters.

When The Kid and his brother John were accused of what they claimed was a trumped-up charge of branding cattle not their own, it was Pike who as deputy sheriff escorted the boys to Fort Benton for trial. While they were in chains in jail Landusky beat them up and the quarrel went beyond any possibility of peace. The brothers were eventually released for lack of proof of guilt and went home shortly before Christmas bound to vengeance.

Christmas was celebration time as active mining was limited by severe freezing weather and the men had time and the inclination to let off pent-up steam. Landusky was determined to celebrate this 1894 Christmas as usual in spite of the feud. The big party lasted two days with men coming to town from all corners of the Little Rockies for the "big free feed and drinks". At the dance, held in the

HIP-ROOFED BARN is one of original buildings on Landusky ranch. While "Montana zephyrs" have blown off some boards and battens they have been replaced with modern, round-headed nails. Others retain old hand-forged type with square heads offering proof of age. Present owner of ranch, friendly, red-headed Pole Thomas Kolczak, attempted to persuade pair of geese to pose properly in center of picture but willful birds persisted in walking out. Tom and wife Jane made author welcome, pointed out where Landusky home stood near spring few hundred feet above barn.

THIS WAS LANDUSKY'S BUGGY. Of it, Tom Kolczak says: "It was stored in the barn and was in perfect shape all these years until this spring. Then one day I found my kids had pulled it outside and almost dismantled it before I caught them. I hope it can be put together because I understand Kid Curry and Landusky often rode together in it before they quarreled."

Curry barn where Loney led the fiddlers, all gunmen were required to check their weapons at the door and they were not returned until the evening of December 26.

The next morning was very cold and snow lay deep. Men drifted aimlessly, most of them drawn to the comforting warmth of the saloons, particularly Jew Jake's. Jake Harris had been in a gun fight with the marshall of Great Falls, losing a leg, and got around with a crutch and sometimes his inverted shotgun. The saloon doubled as a general store displaying all types of merchandise in the rear.

Jake was not surprised to see his friend Pike Landusky come in for a drink but he did look apprehensively toward the store section where Loney and one of the ranch men were looking at a saddle. Landusky ordered a whiskey and was filling his glass when Kid Curry walked in the saloon and slapped him hard on the back.

Landusky twisted around and took a heavy blow on his fragile jaw, falling to the floor. At this point Loney and the hand came up, drew their guns and told the assembling crowd not to interfere. The Kid jumped on the fallen man and began to beat him unmercifully. Pike was unable to ward off the blows clad as he was in a heavy fur overcoat. Although he called for help and a friend, Tom Carter, asked Loney to stop his brother, the Kid continued to beat Pike's face into pulp, then let him up. Somehow Pike managed to draw his gun and pull the trigger. When it failed to fire Kid Curry drew his own .45 and blazed away.

The Kid who might have stayed to plead self-defense, chose instead to flee, thinking perhaps of his shady record. He escaped to join outlaws who were refugees of the Johnson County cattle wars and a gang including Butch Cassidy and the Sundance Kid.

On July 31, 1901, the gang was involved in a sensational train robbery, Kid Curry boarding the train and blowing the safe with dynamite. At least one of the gang was later apprehended and jailed but the rest got away. The Kid began to drink more heavily and was spotted in a saloon in Knoxville, Tennessee. Two officers tried to arrest him but he wounded them both and broke away. Shortly after he was caught and jailed but after several months in a cell he fashioned a noose from a piece of wire, dropped it over the head of his jailer and escaped. The law lost track of him then, presuming he got away to South America to join Cassidy and the Sundance Kid. Or he may have been the Harvey Logan who died of pneumonia in a Denver hospital in 1911.

John Curry remained in charge of the ranch in Landusky, for a while peaceably. Then he — the black-haired and blue-eyed one — fell in love with a widow who returned his affections. The lady attempted to persuade her dead husband's partner, Jim Winters, to sign over to her his share of their ranch. To help matters along, John rode up to Winters' home one day, his gun handy. Winters saw him coming and readied his shotgun. John fired first but missed. His skittish horse began to buck, exposing him to a fatal blast from Winters' gun. John was buried in the regular town cemetery.

Loney had continued to pay court to Landusky's step-daughter now that her protector was dead. In common law fashion the two lived in a cabin in town. When the woman tried to pass a bill in a general store in Fort Benton, it was identified as one stolen in a recent robbery, and Loney made a hurried visit to an aunt in Missouri. Pinkerton men trailed him and surrounded the house, some miles from Kansas City. Loney spotted them and made a dash through the cornfield, receiving a bullet in the head.

Years have passed since Landusky's violent days. Gone with hot-headed gunmen are most of the buildings, lost to decay, fire and vandalism. Enough old structures remain to give some semblance to Main Street but definite identification is doubtful as the few modern residents do not agree. One just knows this was the violent, colorful Montana that was.

RUBY GULCH, MONTANA

Because Ben Phillips was a man of integrity and courage, he buried his two companions killed by the Indians at the risk of his own life. Because his life was spared he sent a letter to the parents of the slain men in England. Because these English people were grateful to Ben for his humane efforts they sent him a check for $2,000 . . . and this tidy sum was the nucleus of the fortune Phillips later made.

The Indian raid took place in the Ruby Gulch area of the Bear Paw Mountains west of the Little Rockies where Phillips and his two partners were prospecting — the same country covered earlier by Tom Carter and John Throop — immediately above the town of Zortman.

With his $2,000 Ben D. Phillips joined forces with Charles Whitcomb and others to buy the August mine at Zortman and the Ruby Gulch mine. Whitcomb's stake was prize money for winning a foot race. The others were Louis Goslin, Coburn brothers, Marlow and Smith, Helena bankers. Whitcomb also developed the Beaver Creek mine farther up the canyon from the Ruby Gulch property and this would become the third largest in the Little Rockies group.

The Ruby Gulch property had a lead 600 feet long, 75 to 127 feet wide, the deposit high on an almost inaccessible shoulder of rocky ground. Finding the vein all but impossible to mine by con-

ORE LADEN CARS emerged from mouth of tunnel to be towed over narrow tracks to mill about ¼ mile distant, route covered by snow sheds. Ruby Gulch is on private, posted property and watchman living in cottage just inside gate graciously gave author permission to explore and photograph relics.

SPIDERY TRESTLE once carried ore cars from tunnel's mouth to mill, passing over road at this point. Steel rails are long gone. Log bunkers more or less successfully hold waste dumps away from road. Hill in background is covered with second growth pines, slowly recovering from many disastrous forest fires. Bisecting road led to "glory hole" where gold lode was exposed.

ventional methods, the owners decided on a combination "glory hole" and tunnel method. The vein was exposed in an open pit, ore removed from the side through a tunnel. By this time electricity was available and the haulage tunnel was equipped with electric locomotive trolley line haulage systems.

A typical month saw 19,000 tons of ore mined and milled. Costs were $1.05 per ton, leaving a profit of $15,000 a month and each month seeing dividends paid to stockholders. During the period the last mill operated, prior to its destruction by fire, 1,000,500 tons of ore were put through it, yielding dividends of 1 million paid to Phillips, Whitcomb and a few minor stockholders. During the early 1920s when labor, machinery and material costs began to skyrocket, the mines and mills were shut down. During this period the mill burned to the ground and Phillips died.

His interests then were sold to St. Paul capitalists, who though wealthy, seemed to take no interest in further development of the mine or granting options to men who were interested, at what they thought were reasonable figures. Then Mose Zimmerman, main stockholder in St. Paul died, leaving the First National Bank and Trust Co. as executor. The bank proved slightly easier to deal with and after three months of negotiations, in December 1934, Carl J. Trauerman, Butte mining engineer, obtained an 18-month option on the mine. He wrote: "High grade ore was opened north of the main Ruby glory hole and additional claims taken up. This high grade ore came from a new and unexpected source. The first car contained 16½ tons of clayey gangue, containing more than 20% moisture. This clay contained manganese oxide, fluorite of a purplish color and gold telluride. The 16½ tons gave net smelter returns of $10,183. Further cars of rich ore were shipped and are still being shipped, and a rich body of ore was opened up in the Alabama claim."

The 18-month option was exercised and paid for in five months and in June Trauerman was elected president of the company. In September of 1935 Whitcomb purchased sufficient stock to bring the Whitcomb-Trauerman interests to 98%. A new

tunnel 400 feet long was being driven to tap high grade ore at a depth of 160 feet. The Ruby Gulch Co. was completing a new mill of 300-ton daily capacity with plans to enlarge to 1,000 tons daily. During this optimistic period Trauerman wrote further: "The company has indicated at least 10 million tons and probably closer to 15 million tons of milling ore that should net a profit of better than $1.00 per ton at the present price of gold".

The following summer a disastrous fire started near Landusky, spreading across the mountains and almost consuming the town. The blaze was started by a cigarette-smoking miner who fell asleep in bed. Since there was no phone at Zortman, a fire guard named Otis Pewitt, who had already been on duty twenty-four hours, drove to Harlem, forty-five miles, to get help for the three hundred Indian fire fighters. When the new group arrived it was trapped in a gully when the fire crowned in the tree tops and created a vacuum at the ground. Near suffocation, the men found a cave but only nine men could crowd into it. Left outside were Dr. S. H. Brockunier, Cameron Baker, John Rowles and Pewitt. When a down draught of super-heated air struck the group all but Pewitt were incinerated. His clothes were burned from him and all skin but the soles of his feet scorched. He later died of cancer, attributed to smoke and heat damage to throat and lungs. The fire started July 25 and burning through 23,000 acres of lodgepole pines, was finally controlled on July 27.

Trauerman's predictions of a permanently rosy future for his mines and the camp of Ruby Gulch were never to come true for 1942 brought the U.S. Government order L.208 which forced all gold

ABANDONED ORE CARS, scattered in disarray on spur of tiny rail line, were towed by mules in early days to machine shops (left) for servicing, in more recent times by small electric locomotives, power coming from coal and water plants below near Zortman.

mines to close. The order was catastrophic for such one-industry towns as Landusky, Zortman and Ruby Gulch. With the closure of the mines inhabitants gradually drifted away to other jobs even to the coastal shipyards, the gold camps soon attaining ghost town status. The mines and mills of Ruby Gulch are guarded by a watchman who says the whole setup could begin operation in two weeks if the price of gold would advance enough to make it pay.

OVERALL VIEW OF RUBY GULCH taken from near mill. Spaces between buildings were once filled with stores, houses. Abandoned schoolhouse stands near exact center of picture. At extreme upper left is "glory hole" from which ore was drained out at bottom through long horizontal tunnel opening at left, behind trees. Here also were located mine offices, blacksmith and machine shops, most still standing in fair condition since mine operated until 1942.

Inquiring at Zortman about road up Ruby Gulch, author was told: "Very simple. You just drive down that dirt road there until you reach the gulch which is filled with tailings. Drive out on them and head up the canyon until you see a gap in the trees. Go through that and you'll pick up the road again. It's steep and rough but I think you can make it." Road levels off just below town, is here seen entering at lower right.

ZORTMAN, MONTANA

Well documented is the story of Bill Hamilton, noted frontiersman, and his party which found gold in the Little Rockies in the late '60s. One of the men, William Bent, left a written record: "In the fall of 1868 they began hiring men at Fort Benton to build Fort Browning on People's Creek in the Milk River country. This was about the fourth of August. After the fort was finished there were too many men and we were told to look out for ourselves. Bill Hamilton, one of the men said 'Boys, suppose we go into the Little Rockies and hunt for gold.' Bill would not work at the fort, as he would not work at anything like that. He was trapping and hunting most of the time. We formed a party with Bill as the leader. Bill, Joe Wye, Fred Merchant, John Thomas, myself and three other men made up the party. This was in the fall of 1868.

"We went around on the east end of the mountains and prospected Dry Beaver. We found gold, but not in paying quantities, and that was, to my knowledge, the first gold found in the Little Rockies."

"I heard once, through a man named Grinnel, that some men who had been mining in the west, went east, and on their return got off the boat and went into the Little Rockies and were never heard of afterwards. Grinnel later was killed by the Indians.

"We kept on prospecting but the ground froze up on us in the fall of '68 before we could do very much, and we threw everything in the mining line away. Bill Hamilton was not very religious, and when the ground froze up he cussed like I never heard a man cuss before. We killed some elk and packed the skins to Fort Benton. I stayed there and took some supplies back for wolfing on the Milk river. All of us who had been in the Little Rockies, excepting Joe Wye who wouldn't come, went on the wolfing party on the upper Milk river into the Piegan country."

After this there is a long gap in the records until those of the big finds of 1884 that brought 2,000 men into the district. Later, old Billy Skillen the "Sage of Fort Belknap," told that story. "On the third of July, 1884, Bill McKinzie stole 'Spud' Murphy's horse down on the Missouri river and started for Fort McGinnis, 65 miles away. Lee Scott, at Rocky Point, started to look for McKinzie and the blue mare he had stolen. The report of the theft

got to the cowboys, and they got McKinzie close to McGinnis, shot him and hung him up on a big cottonwood tree about a mile and a half below the fort on Hancock Creek.

"About July fourth there happened to be some trouble between a white man and a breed at the races over some betting. The white man's name was Rattlesnake. He knocked the breed down, made him apologize and give back the money he had taken. Then the two rode to Reed's Fort in the Judith, or Lewistown, went into the saloon to get a drink, first tying their horses to the rack outside. When they came outside, the citizens thinking they were a tough outfit, which they were, opened fire on them. Rattlesnake and one bystander was killed. From this time on, the 'strangling' of horse thieves and road agents started through northern Montana and the Missouri river country.

"At this time Dutch Louie ran a ranch on Crooked Creek where these toughs would stop, going from the Missouri River and back and forth. Suspicion fell on Louie and the 'stranglers' as the vigilantes were called, got after him. So he went into the Little Rockies with Frank Aldrich and Pike Landusky. They prospected for gold and found

TYPICAL OF OLD BUILDINGS remaining in Zortman is this cabin, occupied until recently. Hardy hollyhocks persist in blooming unattended, year after year. Members of mallow family, these durable plants have such unlikely relatives as Rose of Sharon, cotton and exotic, tropical hibiscus.

some in a creek which they named Alder . . . . Frank Aldrich, who was with Pike Landusky and Dutch Louie when gold was discovered, says they were not the first to discover gold in the Little Rockies, as near the mouth of the gulch where they were working was a pit 100 feet long, by 150 feet wide, that had evidently been sluiced out years before. This discovery was made on Beauchamp's creek.

"Quartz was soon found and then quartz mining began to take the attention of the miners. Soon large mills were reducing the ore, but little real headway was made until the new process was developed for the reduction by cyanide. That was when real wealth began to pour out of the Little Rockies. Thus it was through the fact Dutch Louie was hiding out from the vigilantes that the wealth of the Little Rockies was discovered."

Pete Zortman entered the picture in the 1890s when he located a rich claim on the eastern side of the Little Rockies, the lode that was to become the famous Alabama mine. Doubt is cast on Zortman's making the discovery in an item in the LITTLE ROCKIES MINER of July 4, 1907: "The Alabama was sold by the original locator for $40 to Spaulding, who later interested Pete Zortman and Putnam,

both of Chinook. They did development work and got some ore yielding as high as $2,800 a ton at the Great Falls smelter and one lot of 1,600 pounds returned $6,000."

Yet facts do show Zortman and George P. Putnam owning the mine in 1893 and that the two brought in promoter E. W. King of Barnes-King Co. and Kendall to aid them in forming the Alder Gulch Mining Co. By the turn of the century the rapidly expanding firm was operating the Pole Gulch complex of mines above the now booming town of Zortman. Many improvements followed rapidly. One of them, a 100-ton cyanide mill, built on the only available level ground, proved to be too remote from the mines and hauling expenses forced its closure after a few seasons.

1906 saw the organization of a new concern, The Little Rockies Exploration Co. which took over the defunct mines and mill. The new operators solved the haulage problem by installing an elaborate aerial tramway connecting the mill to the Alabama mine. The town of Zortman then began a lengthy period of prosperity which was increased and extended by the development of still richer mines in Ruby Gulch above Zortman.

SPACES BETWEEN BUILDINGS in Zortman are now wide, many having burned or fallen down. Little church on hill has been kept in repair, services held periodically. Zortman lies at abrupt edge of eastern Little Rockies, outcroppings beyond church rising sharply from level foreground. Zortman and its mines had abundant electricity after pioneer period, power plant burning 70 tons of coal every 24 hours. Current was supplemented by wheel generator operated by water from hot springs near Morrison Butte.

WARREN, IDAHO

Warren, the man, discovered the gold but the story of Warren, the town, revolves more around Judge Poe, Three-Fingered Jack, Cougar Dave, the slave girl, Polly Bemis, and a sluice box full of other characters in the mining camp who saw life scraped raw.

In August of 1862, a party of three — James Warren, Matthew Bledsoe and one Reynolds — left Lewiston to explore the wilderness of the Salmon River basin north and east of Payette Lakes. In less than a month they were back in town with news that turned the careers of hard working, honest men, news of finding rich placer deposits in a swale. Later the place would be called Warren's Meadows but there in Lewiston they called it Hell, for they were exclaiming: "Hell! I'm going there!" Many of those that did shared in riches amounting to more than $14 million by 1884.

Among the early arrivals was Judge Poe, the "Judge" perhaps a complimentary title but Poe's legal training was unusual enough to give him some distinction in rough-and-tumble times. With his partner Joseph Haines and a man named White, Poe took a look around the site while good ground was still free for the staking. It was White who saw the possibilities in a washout left by spring freshets at the mouth of a creek — later called Slaughter Creek because of the abattoir built there — when a panful of gravel washed out $1.70 in gold. In a week several hundred miners were working the gulch.

Haines hurried "outside" for supplies, returning with a pack train September 8, 1862. This was the first of a steady string of supply trains to the new camp. Poe and party set up a crude store at the mouth of the creek and other rough structures were soon going up around it. Next fall when most of the occupants were discovered to be "Secesh Doctrinaires", the place was named Richmond. Miners at

the original discovery site switched the name of their collection of log houses from Warren's Meadows to Washington.

This was war time but Idaho Territory was a long way from Chickamauga and the miners were too busy to exchange shots unless it was on the bar of a saloon in glasses. The claims were proving deeper and richer than most of those discovered in the hectic sixties. Paydirt extended sixteen miles along both sides of the stream, assaying $12 to $17 an ounce, and it was this very richness that caused the demise of Richmond. Gold-laden gravels were found to extend under its buildings, so they were razed and rebuilt in Washington, the ground mined.

In his history of Idaho, Judge Poe related an incident in the camp that came very close to a lynching. "The most serious difficulty which I remember, grew out of a robbery which took place during the winter following the opening of the mines. While Mike Reynolds, one of the miners, was at work near the creek, someone went into his cabin and carried off four or five hundred dollars worth of gold dust. Two men, whose names I cannot now recall, were arrested. I was appointed to defend one and Charles McKay the other.

"That evening while I was sleeping, Three-Fingered Jack, my partner, came to my room and aroused me, telling me that the miners' meeting in which I should be interested was in progress across the street in a saloon. I hurriedly dressed and went to the place indicated. I found it crowded with men eagerly discussing the question of hanging my client. Strangely enough, McKay was one of those ardently supporting this extreme measure. His client was not there, nor was there any talk of punishing him, but when I arrived preparations had already begun for the summary execution of my man.

"I straightway mounted a counter and began an impassioned plea for the poor fellow's life, the re-

ROAD TO WARREN passes along west side of Payette Lake, one of many in area and one of extensive group draining south into Snake River near city of Payette. Warren road passes over drainage divide, entering Salmon River basin near Burgdorf Resort. All of many streams and lakes in Warren district drain generally north into Salmon River. Area is extremely mountainous, heavily timbered, annual snowfall reaching many feet in depth.

sult of which was, that either on my own personal account, or through compassion for the accused, incited by my words, the rope was laid aside and the man held for civil trial. He was afterward convicted and sentenced to a short term in the penitentiary. The discovery of the mines in Montana had drawn away the rough element before the importance of the Warren Mine had been established".

By 1872 Poe had been admitted to the bar and was actively practicing law in Warren, Florence, another big mining camp, and Mount Idaho, its supply center. In '76 he was elected district attorney for the First Judicial District of the Territory and re-elected for the following term. By '88 he had become a member of the Territorial Legislature and had practically given up his working connections with the gold fields.

The autobiography of early day merchant Alonzo Brown sheds some light on how Warren got its groceries. "In the spring there was quite a lot of

miners there and some good mines, and scarcely no provisions there. So Stearns went out to Slate Creek and brought our pack train in over the snow, which would bear a horse in the morning, and we loaded part of the horses with provisions we thought would be needed in Warren's, and Stearns went over with them. He found Warren's a good place to sell our surplus stock and he rented a building and started a store and sent the train back for me to load. We kept the trains running between Florence that summer. Stearns sold goods in Warren's for a fair profit and I sold them in Florence at a loss, sometimes half of the cost and freight. At the end of the second year we came out about even."

Alonzo must have given second thought to his ledger, because in the fall of 1863, he closed out the Florence operation, increased his pack train to a full four-man train, thirty-two pack animals and a saddle horse for each man. He loaded the new outfit at Lewiston, took it into Warren, continuing the run into December when annually heavy snows laid up the outfit.

Prices on all commodities were high in apparent imbalance sometimes. A morning paper from the city brought $1.50 when only two weeks old, but pork was considered exhorbitant at 25c a pound. Hairpins cost Mrs. Schulz, the boarding house proprietor, 75c a dozen, while beef was 15c a pound. Mrs. Schulz charged $3 per meal, and when customers protested this was high, she would bring out her bill for hairpins while not disclosing her butcher bill.

By 1868 the county seat had been moved from its first location at the earlier Florence to "Washington in Warren's Camp." Court records for the next seven years refer to "The Court House in Washington, Idaho County." In 1877 the county seat was moved again, this time to Mount Idaho. Then all use of the name Washington seems to have been discontinued, the camp referred to as Warren's, and a few years later the 's was also dropped.

The camp was filled with picturesque figures, such as Three-Finger Jack, born Sylvester Smith, partner of Judge Poe. While talking with a friend beside a rail fence, Sylvester relaxed by placing his hand over the muzzle of his shotgun, the stock of which rested on the ground. His foot slipped off the lower rail, knee hitting the trigger and firing the gun, changing his name to Three-Finger. Although he made as much as $1,000 a day during his best years in Florence and Warren, he was destitute when he died. Friends cut a section from an old sluice box and closed the ends, making a coffin for him. His son Henry, who recounted these details of his father's life, was the first white child born in Warren, never wore shoes until nearly grown and had only gunny sack shirts most of his life. Henry died in Boise in 1942.

Dave Lewis was a packer who lost so many horses to cougars that he swore vengeance against the depredators and spent the rest of his life killing them. This dedicated warfare lasted until, as he said: "The country got too crowded." As civilization continued to encroach on Cougar Dave, he kept moving to wilder areas. At length he fell ill, hiked from his cabin near Edwardsburg to Boise and entered the veterans' hospital. It was the first time in fifty years he had been in one and he stayed only twenty-four hours, dying of a heart attack. Cougar Dave had reached the age of ninety-two. The previous summer he was asked how many cougars he had killed. "I don't rightly know," he answered. "Years ago I kept track up to two hundred and fifty, then I quit counting."

But most of the stories about Warren characters concern Polly Bemis, the little Chinese wife of Charles A. Bemis. The Orientals here as in most mining camps were industrious and frugal, content to work the dumps scorned by whites and performing most of the menial jobs like running "wash houses". The Grangeville FREE PRESS often carried items about them. One of Sept. 2, 1887: "The Chinese in Warren camp had a grand festival last Sunday, the occasion being the feeding of the dead. Several hogs and chickens were barbecued and taken to the burying ground and were then brought back to make a repast for the living."—of April 10, 1924: "Wrinkled and bent with age but with the enthusiasm of youth, Goon Dick, veteran Idaho miner, arrived in Grangeville Sunday on his annual pilgrimage to the placer mines near Warren. Every spring he goes to Warren, armed with pick, shovel, pan and grubstake to sift the sands for nuggets and dust." Perhaps the last item about these Chinese was on Feb. 15, 1934: "Ah Can, aged Chinese of Warren, was brought out to the county hospital Tuesday by Chuck Walker, pilot of the McCall-Warren plane. The trip was made in a little over a half hour."

Many of the stories about Polly Bemis are conflicting but as to her coming to Warren, she tells of it in an interview by Countess Gizicka for FIELD AND STREAM of July, 1921. In the writer's words: "She stands not much over four feet, neat as a pin, wrinkled as a walnut, and at sixty-nine is

GENERAL VIEW OF WARREN backstreets from one of many high mine dumps edging town. Several cabins are occupied in summer by vacationers and few attendants in tavern, small grocery, gas pump. Many buildings have survived due to occasional resurgences of mining, when roofs were replaced and repairs made.

DISTINCTIVE ARCHITECTURE of several buildings in Warren is represented in this structure facing main street. It served as grocery store during active period of dredging in '40s, as saloon in earlier days, was reported "fanciest drinking emporium in town."

full of dash and charm . . . Polly told me . . . 'My follucks in Hong Kong had no grub. Dey sell me, slave girl. Old woman, she smuggle me into Portland. I cost $2,500. Don't looka it now! Old Chinese man, he took me along to Warrens in pack train."

Not mentioned are details of how she met and married Charlie Bemis. One version has it he won a poker game at the saloon where Polly worked, that the dainty miss herself was the prize, that a quarrel broke out between Bemis and an admirer of the girl, John Cox, a halfbreed Indian, that Cox shot Bemis putting out his right eye.

There is a variation to the fight story. Cox and Bemis were playing poker in the saloon, the Chinese girl present when the argument started. Cox fired at Bemis, the bullet entering the eye socket but not

LITTLE POLLY BEMIS was beloved by everyone in Warren in a day when Orientals were not popular. She came to America as slave girl from China, passed her youth as song and dance girl in saloons of raw mining camp of Warren. As charms faded she married Charlie Bemis, who may have won her in a poker game or fallen in love with her as she nursed his wounds received in gun fight. (Photo courtesy Idaho Historical Society)

the eye itself. Polly immediately took Bemis in charge, "cleaning out the wound with a crochet hook", it is said. A doctor came from Grangeville to tend the wound which Polly had cleaned and dressed. The jolting the doctor got on the rough road put him in a vile humor and he is reported to have taken one look at the eye, proclaimed the case hopeless, denounced all connected with the affair, collected $500 for his trouble and departed in a rage.

Polly then continued nursing Bemis, saved the eye, and in due time married her patient. One old timer reported the whole thing in a nutshell: "Well, poker had something to do with it. Warren was a wild town in those days and gold dust and poker chips seemed to reach out towards each other. . . . I guess the fact was that Bemis did get hurt in a poker game, Polly nursed him back to health, and nature and a minister did the rest."

After some years of living at Warren the couple moved to a ranch on the Salmon River where they welcomed all comers until the death of Bemis in 1922. Next year the little widow was taken on a trip to Grangeville, where for the first time in her life she saw automobiles and movies. Before her death at eighty-one she requested she be buried where she could still hear the roar of the foaming Salmon River.

Only the famous Florence (now reported razed to the ground and the site inaccessible) surpassed Warren as a quartz mining area. Hard rock mining began in 1867, and that same year the Rescue Mine turned out $13,000, mostly in gold, with some silver (present in some degree in most of the deep mines at Warren.)

Around 1870 things were quiet at Warren, activity starting up again about '73, when deep shafts of the Rescue, Samson, Charity and Keystone began producing heavily. At the turn of the century the town was almost dormant again, renewed activity starting in 1915 with a report from the state inspector of mines "A great revival of lode mining activity and interest was manifested at Warren placer district . . . as the result of successful development of ore shoots in the old Rescue Mine at considerable depths through a lower tunnel."

This burst too, died down in a few years, to be reactivated by new type dredging operations, reaching a peak around 1938. There was also some ore removal from several of the old shafts, including the historic Rescue, which was the deepest in Idaho during its peak of production. With the stabilizing of gold prices, Warren like hundreds more gold camps, settled into the doldrums. Reached best from McCall, the camp is well preserved and not too greatly altered.

ALEC BEETON'S PLACE, about 11 miles below Warren, was way station on stage road to mining camp. This was central building of group—hotel, dining room, tavern. Projecting roof enabled stage coaches to drive to front door under shelter from rain, snow. Area was logged off years ago, second growth trees mostly jack pine.

MOUNT IDAHO, IDAHO

It just don't pay, California Joe said, to trust everybody. Especially when you've got a cabin on a pack train trail to a mining camp, set out victuals and put people up for the night. Now take that halfbreed feller.

California Joe's blooded Kentucky mare was tethered outside the cabin when the halfbreed rode up. He tied his scrawny cayuse next to the mare, had supper and was up early, saying he'd settle his bill after breakfast. The next thing California Joe knew was both the breed and the mare had disappeared. But what the breed didn't know was California Joe, whose real name was Mose Milner. Grabbing a rifle and another horse, he took a short cut to a wooded clump on the trail and sure enough, here came the renegade. Up came the rifle and one bullet into the fellow's skull finished him. California Joe left the body on the trail with a message: "Warning to horse thieves. Mose Milner, Mount Idaho."

About 1860 this wanderer built a log cabin in a meadow filled with beautiful spikes of blue flowers for which Camas Prairie was named, and the bulbs of which were staple food for the Indians. Milner's cabin was a "double" with a second halfstory on the route to the fantastically booming mining camp of Florence. Then with the help of a partner named Francis he brushed out forty-five miles of pack train trail and collected tolls for its use, finishing the project in the spring of 1862. As travel increased Milner finished the upper floor of the cabin and added a wing, serving meals to sojourners at a dollar each, giving one away now and then if a man was broke. But Milner suffered permanent damage to his health in an encounter with a mountain lion and was forced to sell his toll road and cabin.

The man who bought the property was Loyal P. Brown who became Mount Idaho's leading citizen for the rest of his long life. Making the trail stop on his way to look into prospects in Florence and hearing the cabin was to be sold, he talked the matter over with another traveler, James Odle, with the result that they went partners, Brown trading his two mares for squatters' rights to the land and hotel, Odle filing on the land just west of it. After three years Brown bought out his partner and on the combined tract most of the town of Mount Idaho was built. The timber-covered mountain at the southern edge of Camas Prairie had been called Mount Idaho since the discovery of the Florence mines and Brown applied the name to his town.

He gave the name Luna to the hotel and Mrs. Brown did the cooking. She did not like the English gang of outlaws that worked the Florence trail although she admitted young Dave English was "right handsome". What bothered her most was their target practice in the yard. One bullet pinged into her kitchen between the logs, scattering chunks of clay chinking into the bowl when she was kneading bread. That kind of nonsense could spoil her reputation as a cook if she didn't get every last piece out.

The gang would run up a sizeable bill at times but Dave English always paid up after a foray on the trail. One traveler related he had been held up just out of town by a lone bandit, a member of the gang. "You're too late," he told the outlaw. "Another robber hit me up the line and took everything I had, even my tobacco money." The man with the gun gave him a dollar and a grin. But the Robin Hoodish "reign of terror" was short lived. An entry in the old Luna ledger of November 9, 1862 noted: "Dave English and his men Peebles and Scott were hanged at Lewiston a few days ago."

A post office was established in the town about 1862, with Frank Fenn as post master, then Loyal Brown. In 1873 a larger building replaced the original hotel of Mose Milner and a stage line established a route from Lewiston to the town. In 1875 Vollmer and Scott started a store to compete with Rudolph's pioneer mercantile. These buildings, with

LOYAL P. BROWN established home in wilderness that would be town of Mount Idaho. Later, during Nez Perce War which raged around the edges of his town, he turned over his hotel for use as hospital for care of casualties from Battle of White Bird Canyon. (Photo courtesy Idaho Historical Society).

a group of residences, made up most of Mount Idaho when the Nez Perce War broke out.

After many rumors and warnings, to which Mount Idaho became inured, some citizens not even believing a struggle was going on, the dark period came when Chief Joseph carried the war into the White Bird region. About two hundred and fifty terrified prairie people flocked into the town for protection. This was on the evening of June 14 and they remained until Joseph and his hordes of braves pulled out of the area. But now Mount Idaho knew there was war.

The first action was to build a makeshift fort on a small hill at the edge of town. Two parallel rail fences were rigged up to a height of five feet in an incomplete circle about a hundred and fifty feet across, space between rails filled with brush, rocks and even sacks of flour. A narrow access passage toward the west was left open as it seemed no attack would come from that direction.

Some wounded victims of the White Bird raids were brought into Mount Idaho at intervals, among them seven-year-old Maggie Manual, carried in by young Patrick Price. The dead and wounded from the Cottonwood battle flooded the limited facilities and the hotel was turned into a hospital. Mr. Morris of Lewiston arrived to take charge, bringing a number of nurses. The dead were buried in the Mount Idaho cemetery.

Lewis Rice, fifty-nine, friend of all in the Mount Idaho area, who know him as Bude, tells of his grandmother who was called Mona by the Indians, and of her experiences at the time. "She was walking down the road real slow because she was going to have a baby almost any minute when an Indian on a horse came tearing along, his hair streaming out behind him. 'Mona', he hollered, 'get up fort quick! Nez Perce go to war on whites. My friends, no want get um hurt!' Mona hurried as fast as she could to

STONE MONUMENT was erected and dedicated June 31, 1939, by townspeople on site of fort built for protection against Indians in Nez Perce War. Almost every person in small remnant of Mount Idaho and interested former residents of Grangeville contributed to casting of bronze plate commemorating tragedy. Not long after placement on monument it was pried off by vandals. Fort was hastily thrown together—150 foot circle of parallel rail fences, space between rails filled with rocks, etc. It stood in meadow directly behind tree and faint traces can be seen on close examination.

WHEN LOYAL P. BROWN was near death he requested burial under group of trees on his property. His wife was later buried there, marble headstone erected for both. In later years area became pasture, heavily overgrown with brush. About 1955, Mrs. Daisy Smith, daughter of the Browns, distressed over wild condition of graves and constant invasion by cattle, had parents' remains removed to regular cemetery and modern markers installed. Original headstones were left where pushed over at time of exhumation. Mrs. Smith has since passed away, joining her parents in cemetery.

LAST HOME OF PIONEER Loyal P. Brown, "Father of Mount Idaho". While he exerted benevolent, protective influence over town, he did not favor progress, refused to sell his large property holdings. Period of prosperity following Nez Perce struggle was smothered for lack of space for outside investors. Advantage was taken by Grangeville, now thriving town.

warn the other settlers, then walked up the steep hill to the fort. She tried to help the others pile up sacks of flour and it wasn't long before her baby was born, right there in the fort. That was Walter, my father, and I was born here in Mount Idaho too, just at the bottom of the hill where the fort was."

The period following the war, from about 1878 to 1880, the town had its greatest prosperity and highest population. Loyal Brown erected a steam-powered sawmill close to town, logs hauled to it by oxen, and it cut 12,000 feet a day. The Idaho County Courthouse and Masonic Hall were built of Brown's lumber as was a stout jail next to the court-house. In 1896 the sawmill and flour mill next to it burned to the ground.

After 1880 Mount Idaho declined, one factor more than any other being Loyal Brown's refusal to let outsiders buy land. He had been a great benefactor to the community but now was willing to lease only. The town's big opportunity passed by when Brown turned down a request by newspaper man A. F. Parker to buy a central parcel of land and put up a printing plant. Instead it went to Grangeville which forged ahead and is today the leading town in the area. Mount Idaho faded away to a mere remnant, rich in history only.

Bude Rice tells of his little sister "When I was a kid of ten or so, Mount Idaho still had quite a few Chinamen, left over from the old days. They were all pretty ancient by then and one we called Old Cann must have been around eighty. His prized possession was a beautiful diamond ring. He always said he had won it fair and square in a poker game. He was very fond of my little sister Sadie and when she was around five, he gave her the ring. She was never very strong and a year later she died. At the funeral my mother said to my dad: 'We really ought to take that diamond ring off and have it for a keepsake.' Old Cann heard it and spoke right up. 'No takee off ring. I give, she have, she keep.' So little Sadie was buried over there on the hill with her diamond ring still on her finger."

The old cemetery is one of Mount Idaho's most interesting features. Not much else remains. Loyal P. Brown's home still stands, smothered by tall grass, weeds and decrepit fruit trees. On the opposite hill is a rock monument put up by local citizens to mark the spot where the old fort stood, the original bronze plaque since carried off by vandals. Nearby is the site of the first grade school and the one built to replace it. At the crossroads just below stood Mount Idaho's pride, the court-house, and across the street was the large log building which housed the pack train outfitters store. Next to it was the saloon where drivers took several for the long trail to the Florence mines. This was the bustling center of Mount Idaho but it is very quiet now.

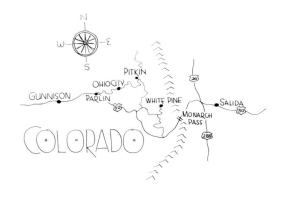

PITKIN, COLORADO

Ladies were rare enough in early mining camps, especially those who backed up their forthright ideas with guns. In Pitkin "Captain" Jack, whose given name was Ellen E., had the temperament of a tarantula and was further poison with a pair of six-guns.

Thoroughly unpredictable, she might appear in men's rough pants and jacket or dressed to the hilt of fashion in women's clothes, complete with bustle. In fact the bustle was most important. "Without pants pockets," she retorted with a sting in the words, "where else am I going to carry my money, stocks and diamonds?"

She drove through the streets at top speed, disregarding corners, until one day her carriage overturned, spilling the lady out into the dirt. There she lay unconscious, bustle up — thirty, blonde and blue-eyed. A passel of eager young bucks rushed to her aid. One cried: "Give her air! Another started loosening her dress and suddenly Captain Jack sat up and spewed forth a stream of oaths that were never spoken in her Quaker church. The question whether the man's touch had been on her bodice or bustle was never answered.

A train of burros came through town one day, the little animals braying painfully, and someone told Captain Jack: "That driver always lets the burros' backs get raw and the packs hurt them. But you dassent go and do anything about it. That jay-whacker's got a violent bad temper." But so did the lady. She jerked out her guns, leveled them at the driver, ordered him to remove the packs and held the guns steady until he did.

Ellen Jack was hospitable — up to a point, such

as one she made when a young man moved some supplies to her claim. It was late and when he started to go home, she invited him to stay overnight. The youth saw only one bed in the cabin and whatever hopes or doubts he had were quickly dispelled. "Let's make one thing clear right now," said Captain Jack with the vigor of womanly virtue as she dropped a gun in the middle of the bed. "This is my side. That's yours. See you stay on it."

In his book, DIGGING GOLD AMONG THE ROCKIES, George Thomas Ingham gives an accurate picture of Pitkin in its first hectic years. He arrived in Buena Vista, Colorado, just before the railroad reached that camp on its way to the wildly booming Leadville, and in company with an equally eager friend, visited many of the camps along the East fringe of the Rockies, then went "up and over", emerging at the back door of Pitkin and other camps on the Western side of the range.

"We arrived at Miller's," wrote Ingham, "where there were three or four log cabins about noon, which were the first evidences of civilization, where travelers are lodged and entertained when they wish to stop awhile on their journey. There are two or three mines in the vicinity. The 'Margaret', owned by Miller and Hall, was discovered about a year ago. It seems Miller came along a ledge and camped for the night. Finding float nearby the next morning, he traveled up the hillside for a few rods where he started a tunnel, striking a vein of silver-lead or Galena ore of considerable value. The parties claim to have been offered $20,000 for their find. Quartz Creek is a very rapid stream with a succession of falls and rapids and we descended from

CITY HALL had lower floor carved out of hillside. Upper floor is one large room, was used for lodge meetings, dances, social functions, reached by separate outside stairway. The covered one shown here replaced an older, uncovered one on other side. Building is now unused, the town having only about a dozen residents. Old hotel is at left, service limited to small lunch counter in lobby.

our high elevation to a lower one very fast. When down in the vicinity of Pitkin the mountains rose less abruptly, were not so high and became heavily timbered with a species of yellow pine. . . . . .

"The first evidence of our approach to Pitkin was the site of a steam saw-mill and some log huts in the gulch above town. The valley here widens to ¼ mile or more, and Pitkin is situated on a level grassy flat a mile or more in length. It is a lovely site for a town, being in a grassy park in which there is no timber, yet the surrounding hills are densely covered with spruce, pine to their very tops. Quartz Creek passes on one side close to the mountain, and an irrigating ditch carries the clear

water the entire length of the town along the side of Main Street.

"Main Street is thickly studded with buildings in all stages of erection. Tents and log huts are everywhere to be seen, and for a town of only two or three weeks' growth shows considerable energy in the great number of buildings which have been erected. About five weeks ago three or four log cabins were about the sum total of the buildings in the place. Now corner lots sell for $800. Its elevation is about 9,000 feet.

"One old gentleman who came into town last fall without any means save for his team and less than $100 in cash, purchased nine or ten lots, paying $5 to $10 for each, and holding them until spring, disposal returns ranging from $300 to $750, thereby clearing about $5,000.

"Hotels not being plentiful at the time of our arrival we took quarters at one of the numerous lodging houses which appear to be the fashionable sleeping places of the town. The house in question was a large tent, 18x50 feet; the floor was the ground, which was, however, not level, and was covered with three or four inches of sawdust. A canvas partition divided the sleeping apartment from the rest of the room. There was a stove and numerous boxes and trunks as substitutes for chairs, which constituted the furniture of the room. The bunks on which we slept were made of rough boards,

arranged in a row at the side of the room with two tiers, one above the other, steamboat fashion. The beds consisted of loose hay tossed upon the boards and covered with gray blankets, and comfits were used as covers. No sheets or pillows were to be seen, coats were universally used for pillows. Price of lodging, 50¢.

"We slept well, and in the morning felt refreshed. We went to the 'Bon Ton' for breakfast, where we found two ladies in charge. It was a tent 16x24 with a sawdust floor like our bunk house, and the tables reclining at an angle of about fifteen degrees from the level. However, everything bore the atmosphere of cleanliness and neatness, and we had an excellent breakfast of beefsteak, fried eggs,

BACK YARDS of most abandoned houses are filled with clutter of earlier, busier days.

bacon, fried potatoes, corn bread, warm biscuits, butter and coffee, and in fact everything essential to a good appetite, and well cooked, for a half dollar. We were surprised at such good fare in such a new town, but found it to be the prevailing prices of the place.

"The following day was Sunday, yet the stores and saloons were open; the sounds of the saw and hammer were ringing all day long. Reports of shots from giant powder while blasting in the mines were frequent all day, and the din and rush of travel and freighting through the streets went on as usual. These mining towns have very little regard for the Sabbath.

"Within six weeks there have been erected fifteen hotels, restaurants, lodging houses, and some forty to fifty business houses and saloons. By the 15th of June when a count was taken, there were 1,050 people within the city limits, and doubtless as many more were camping and prospecting within a few miles around the city. There were 168 dwellings, 4 hotels, 8 restaurants, 12 saloons, 50 stores and businesses, a bakery; 80 vacant unfinished buildings, 3 meat markets, several real estate offices and one jail. But with all this population there were but 50 ladies in the town and about 55 children."

Ingham continues with a detailed price list of most commodities in the infant town, including — hay, 5c per pound; butter, 50c; rice, 20c; dried apples, 20c; beefsteak, 20c; coal oil, $1.25 a gallon. He comments that while these prices "may seem high, still it must be taken into consideration that everything must be freighted in from Alamosa." As for the labor and man power situation that first year, Ingham makes it clear that the professional man could not expect to find a comfortable niche, nor could book-keepers or clerks make a lot of money. Carpenters on the other hand, would be welcomed with open arms and purse strings, earning as much as $2.50 for a nine hour day.

By 1880 the town had a newspaper, the PITKIN MINING NEWS, which carried a column of bits and gossip pieces called "Pitkin Pellets". Being of a highly personal nature, not always complimentary to the citizens involved, the editor was often threatened with violent reprisal, but seems to have escaped bodily harm. When the first train came in on July 12, 1882, the paper carried a flamboyant story about the "future growth of our fair city" and witheringly referred to the neighboring camps of Tin Cup and Gothic as being "necessarily temporary since they have no rail service".

The arrival of a train in the mountain camp was indeed something of a miracle. The rails had been extended upward and westward from the eastern slope camps of St. Elmo (then Forest City) and Romley (Murphy's Switch until 1897). As the railroad neared the summit of the range it stopped short of the steepest peaks and dove straight through via an engineering marvel of the day — the Alpine Tunnel. While the tunnel was being bored Pitkin suffered its most violent times. Laborers, released from tunnel work on Saturday night, descended on the saloons and bordellos to whoop it up. They did it so thoroughly citizens locked up doors and windows and went to bed, resigned to the worst.

For a time the rails ended at Pitkin, were later extended to Ohio City, then on down to Parlin where they connected with the Denver and Rio Grande, so that service went all the way to Gunnison. This was a great step forward for the area since the mountain passes were usually closed by snow for eight months. The tunnel itself remained clear but the adjacent slopes presented a constant struggle against snow drifts in fall, winter and spring.

After Pitkin had erected saloons and bawdy houses, someone thought of a theater and built one. Looking around for talent, the owner was informed an engineer in Gunnison, D. J. McCanne, had devised some spectacular stage effects for his amateur production of A DREAM OF FAIRYLAND. McCanne was invited to present the play in the new theater and he accepted without giving much thought to the the matter. An ingenious man, he had rigged up a dynamo powered by a heavy steam pump to provide power for illuminating a series of incandescent lamps. On the stage of the Gunnison playhouse the lighting was successful enough. Concealed in artificial flowers the lamps would light up when the good fairies were on stage, and die down when evil imps appeared. But Pitkin had to get along without all this, the electrical equipment too bulky to transport to the camp. The show must go on, McCanne said, and on the Pitkin stage substituted regular pyrotechnical flares for the bulbs. Everything went fine until the scheduled blaze of light in the flowers. The flash material went off with squeals of delight which quickly became choking coughs as clouds of dense smoke drove the audience outside. Despite theatrical tradition, the show did not go on.

One killing in Pitkin started as a domestic squabble, Tom Sullivan's wife going home to mother. Tom sequestered himself in his home with a bottle to substitute for his wife's affections. "Sullivan tried to drown his sorrows," Betty Wallace,

Gunnison historian observed succinctly, "but succeeded only in nourishing his grievances." The whiskey lasted all day, got Tom roaring drunk and he started for his mother-in-law's with .41 pistol in hand. Deputy Sheriff W. E. Hammon and Jake McWilliams saw him on the run, heard piercing screams in the house. Catching up with Sullivan, they talked him into walking back downtown but neglected to remove his gun.

At first peaceable, Sullivan's mood suddenly made a turn for the worse. He whipped out his gun and fired two shots at Hammon's head, one of them taking deadly effect. McWilliams made a hasty retreat and Sullivan, now master of the situation, paraded up and down Pitkin's main street, chasing everyone to cover. Ammunition exhausted, he fled on horseback up the gulch, pursued by a hastily organized posse. Overtaken in Armstrong Gulch near Tin Cup, he tamely surrendered and since there was a good chance of a lynching if he were held in the Pitkin jail, he was rushed to Gunnison.

In 1891 and 1892 Pitkin hit its peak of prosperity. All mines were producing, the Islet turning out silver bricks weighing 774 ounces and another mine broke into a new vein that poured out still more silver, bringing another influx of miners. Then came the crash of '93, suspending all mining activity. Partial recovery came in '95 when the catastrophe had faded somewhat and Pitkin limped along until a gold strike was reported in the district. When none was discovered nearby, the town suffered another relapse. Pitkin was having a full-fledged depression five years before the general one in the '30s and this was the beginning of a decline that carried into the present time.

Many buildings still stand, the little stream of water referred to by Ingham still sparkling beside Main Street. In the lobby of the otherwise silent old hotel, an enthusiastic young Canadian woman will prepare a meal for the occasional visitor. Surprised by a total of four guests one day recently, she remarked regretfully: "I was thinking this morning of baking a pie. Now I wish I had."

PITKIN IS FULL OF OLD WAGONS, relics of days when all freight was hauled to lofty mining camps by vehicles pulled by as many as ten teams of horses or mules. Pictured in detail is heavy brake shoe used to retard too-rapid descent of wagon on steep hills. Frequently these were augmented by logs dragged along behind.

PITKIN RETAINS many early day buildings, some still occupied in summer. Log construction of this one seems to date it before erection of sawmill, upper facing of boards and battens added later.

WHITE PINE, COLORADO

George S. Irwin was White Pine's alert and imaginative newspaper man although he finally went to jail, his most consistent struggle was with the pack rats. When the WHITE PINE CONE printed its last edition after ten years of lively existence, the furry thieves had made away with everything they could carry or drag except the type lice.

When Irwin, his partner and a printer's devil named George Root arrived in the remote Colorado camp in 1883, they spent their first night in a lean-to adjoining the log cabin where the paper would be printed. The rats were big, noisy and bold and banging a shoe on the floor only made them more active. So young Root grabbed his Wesson .44 carbine from the bunk post and handed it to Irwin below him. The editor heard a crunching sound and blazed away, and "no more was heard save strong men struggling for the word." In the morning Root pried up some floor boards near the body of the victim and found a cache of objects belonging to the previous occupants, among them trunk straps, neckties, dish rags, slippers, forks and spoons.

The WHITE PINE CONE enjoyed a regional reputation for genial reflections on the news and morals of the camp, under the heading — "Little Cones" — material like: "The boys all washed their feet in the Hot Springs Sunday. There will be no fish in Hot Creek this summer" . . . . "We will present a copy of the CONE for one year to the first couple that marries in the gulch between the first and last day of February, proximo. Marriage comes h'gh but we must have one occasionally." . . . "White Pine suffered an agonizing famine this week. For two whole days there was not a drop of whiskey in town. Nothing but a liberal supply of peach brandy and bottled beer prevented a panic."

Seldom was the news reported straight. After many months of snowy winter when supplies were hauled into town on ox-drawn sleds, Irwin cheerfully chronicled the end. "The first wagon over the road between Sargent's and White Pine since last fall was the stage last Friday. It was quite a treat for our people to see once again a wheeled vehicle. The stage will hereafter make regular daily trips."

When times were dull and news scarce, Irwin would improvise as with this tongue-in-cheek report of a hold up, February 15, 1889. "BOLD HOLD UP—THRILLING EXPERIENCE OF PASSENGERS ON THE SARGENT-TOMICHI STAGE LINE.

"Ingold Peterson drove merrily day by day through the dark canyon without thought of disaster. But the events of last Monday are calculated to cause the traveler in the near future to traverse the canyon only with fear and trembling.

"Last Monday was most favorable for a tragedy. For a time dark clouds obscured the sun, and a snowfall darkened the heavens. The atmosphere was gruesome and uncanny. A feeling of depression came over the passengers — a silent premonition of approaching danger.

"On the stage besides the driver, Ingold Peterson, were Joe Domandel, a Miss Lilly Dinkins and an alleged drummer. Let us say right here that suspicion attaches to the drummer. It is even charged directly that he was an accomplice of the hold up, an accessory before the fact. There are

WHEN MAIN STREET of White Pine was lined with business buildings, this peak-roofed one was novelty, as others were all false-fronted. Note evidence of outside stairway indicating close crowding of adjoining buildings. Only few scattered structures remain here now, survivors of fires, weather and old age.

several circumstances since remembered tending to corroborate these charges against the drummer.

"When the stage stopped at Cosden he was seen to go into Pat's Place and emerge a few minutes later with a strong aroma tied to his breath, which kept floating out on the morning breeze. Was this the signal to his pals, watching from some high point?

"He frequently glanced at the mail bags, and nervously watched on either side of the road as the stage entered the narrow canyon.

"It was particularly noticed, also, that just before the stage was attacked, the drummer placed his thumb and forefinger to his nose in a most significant manner.

"Evidently the drummer should have been apprehended. Witnesses will swear, we understand, that they saw the road agent throw something which the drummer caught with the dexterity that comes only with long practice. About midway between Cosden and White Pine as the driver hurried the team around a curve, there suddenly came to view a dark, grim sentinel who stood silently by the side of the road. Not a word was said but his actions were ominous, and the passengers shuddered as the stage drew near.

"Joe Domandel, having the safety of the lazy at heart, begged the driver to stop, but the blood of the Northman was aroused, and like the chieftain warriors of his ancestry, he was resolved to do or die.

" 'Up there, Kalma! On, on Ladoga!' With dilated nostrils and trembling limbs, but obedient to lash and rein the horses sprang forward to face the broadside, well delivered.

"A few sharp screams, muttered curses and stifling gasps, and the danger is past. But the holdup had done his work. Peterson and Carr are badly hit, Domandel and the lady are unharmed, however, and the faithful horses bring the load to White Pine. It was known there the moment the stage came in sight an accident had occurred. There was something in the air that spoke of dire catastrophe. A crowd gathered as the stage approached, but no one remained long, the smellability was offended, and the victims were left to their fate.

"The holdup man escaped and the drummer left. Peterson is recovering, but he tells under the seal of strictest confidence that hereafter he will yell at the first sight of a mean, low down, loaded skunk!"

Irwin's newspaper ceased publication when the editor was sentenced to fifteen months in prison in Laramie, Wyoming for some infraction of the postal laws, presumably in the mailing of his papers. The editor's incarceration began shortly after he and other newspaper men had protested the fact that a notorious murderer had recently escaped lynch mobs through protective efforts of lawmen. Irwin had commented: "We suppose that this killer, like all Gunnison County's bad men with guns, will escape the gallows in the end, and possibly be awarded a leather medal as the champion killer. Sad state of affairs."

Irwin's arrest and conviction provoked further caustic editorial barbs to the effect that the course of justice was pursuing strange ends when a man could be put in jail for a comparatively trivial offense, at the same time allowing cold-blooded murderers to go free.

White Pine's rich silver and lead deposits were first worked around 1878. In a couple of years the camp was flourishing. Some silver was in "native glance" form, some in "wire" formation. One locality, Contact Mountain, was said to be "a mass of magnetic iron pyrites carrying silver." Some of the mines developed were Morning Star, Evening Star, Black Warrior, Copper Bottom and Copper Queen.

White Pine held its first election in 1880. Ballot boxes were made up in town, all possible votes were collected in town, then the boxes were carried up the trail to the next camp, Tomichi. Any miner met passing along the trail was invited to cast his vote. At Tomichi remaining voters cast their votes, the results being sent down to Gunnison which by this time was the county seat.

In the fall of the year before, the area had an Indian scare. The Meeker Massacre of 1879 caused panic among the settlers, even though the Indian Agency had been moved to Uncompahgre. Many camps set up guards, at Gunnison settlers built a small fort on a cliffside, maintaining a guard for several weeks, when fear subsided. At White Pine, some seventy miners with only thirteen guns among them established guard stations on the hills above the camp. Onset of winter snows caused abandonment of the posts by mutual agreement. One man, set to guard the gate at a break in the fence at the edge of town jumped the gun by returning to town before the rest, Reproved, he defended himself. "Well, anyway, I put up the bar before I left."

The spring of 1884 was particularly bad because of avalanches, then generally called "runs." At Woodstock, over the mountain from White Pine one of these slides swept away the little railroad station at a time when people were waiting for the train. Carried away and smothered were fourteen people, including Mr. Doyle and his four children, only Mrs. Doyle surviving. In addition to the station, many other buildings were destroyed, boarding house, telegraph shack and many cabins. The awaited train wouldn't have arrived, as it happened, the entire crew was busy fighting a snow obstruction at Baldwin.

The same day, March 10, an avalanche hit the workings at the Magna Charta tunnel, carrying away most of the buildings, but not causing any loss of life. The CONE carried the story. "The wind blew a veritable hurricane, driving the snow with hurricane force. Tom Farrell and Terry Hughes, employees of the Magna Charta, went to work as usual. They were in the blacksmith shop connected with the tunnel, when about eight o'clock, a huge snow slide came down Granite Mountain with a deafening roar, striking the shop with a fearful impact. Mr. Hughes was driven through a partition

then carried out through the end of the shop and thrown about fifty feet down the mountain side. Fortunately he landed in a bed of soft snow and soon extricated himself. Seeing nothing of Farrel he gave the alarm and some twenty or more men hurried to the scene of the accident and began searching for him. A few minutes later he was found imprisoned under the roof of the shop, but the combined efforts of the men to raise the roof were futile until it was broken to pieces. Farrell was unconscious when taken out, but recovered after a time. Examination showed that aside from a few bruises he was alright." The rescue party had just returned to town when a second and even larger slide swept over the Magna Charta, completing the removal of any buildings its predecessor had neglected.

Fifteen years later, again in March, an even more disastrous slide hit the Magna Charta mine

MANY SMALL "SUBURBS" grew up around White Pine. This one on Tomichi Creek has nearly disappeared, leaving only this small group of buildings. One nearest camera is likely unique, owner adding stucco front to old log cabin.

buildings. This monster removed all obstacles in its path, including a number of cabins. It killed several people. Young M. C. Smith was buried under the rush of snow, but lived to tell about it. "I was eating breakfast in my mother's kitchen. The first thing I saw was the front of the house falling on me. Instantly all was dark, and soon I found myself in a little place where I could sit up. The snow kept settling down around me until only my hands were free. I felt around and found that I was safely hemmed in. I called out but no response. I decided to take things easy, all the time feeling that I would certainly be rescued. At last I heard a noise up above. I gave the miner's rap on the eating table which was holding the debris off me, with a piece of broken plate. The raps were answered. The workmen seemed to redouble their efforts and soon I was free again. Mother was lying on a cot in the dining room sick when she was hit and killed instantly. I was under ten or fifteen feet of snow and remained there 4½ hours."

Little eight-year-old Perry Sweezy in another house had also been with his mother. As the snow hit, he called out to her, heard a muffled response, a groan, then silence. He had no idea how long it was when he heard rescuers digging above, but when he did, he called out, "Boys, can you get me out?" The men heard him, assuring him that they would, and to remain still. His father and older brother had been outside sawing wood. They never had a chance, being overwhelmed with no protection. Mr. C. L. Stitzer and his son Bert were also cutting wood, but they were working on a rise of ground. The descending avalanche divided at the obstruction, roaring around both sides, reforming at its lower end. It was Bert who skied into town to summon help, fear-

BONES OF ONCE HUGE MILL seem to have been ravaged by time and weather rather than usual enemy, fire. Most such mills took advantage of terrain, receiving ore at top level, passing material downward by easy gravity. First level contained heavy crushers, succeeding stages reduced chunks to powder, usually in ball mill, then material was combined with chemicals in tanks, becoming sludge in which metals floated to top as thick foam to be scraped off by revolving paddles and dried, becoming "concentrates" ready for shipment to smelter.

BOARD-EDGE SEAT and shoulder stop of primitive latrine offered ... comfort, discouraged any tendency of miner to gold-brick or ... with others on same errand. Structures were common to ... mills where large numbers of men were employed.

ful every foot of the way of starting another run. The disaster marked the end of the Magna Charta. It had never been a rich producer and as a Jonah for avalanches was closed down for keeps.

In one respect White Pine was certainly unique. Instead of the usual gunfire, quarrels were settled by fisticuffs, or at least some certainly were. Designated for this purpose was a small area just above town. The spot was known as Battle Park because of its frequent use as a ring. Since the men had to be at work in the mines by eight A.M., the bouts had to be staged before breakfast. First of such encounters was what was expected to be a "slugfest" between Charley Harmon and Tom Mourin. Harmon led off with a hard right to Mourin's chin, but it did not connect because of the extreme near sightedness of the aggressor. While trying to regain his balance, he was an easy target for Mourin's hefty punch, a blow that floored Harmon for the count.

The crowd, eager up to this point, booed the contestants, then turned their attentions to the next event, featuring two men who had quarreled over a girl in a saloon the night before, George Church and James Deck. This one lasted three rounds, affording considerable satisfaction to the spectators, who then left contentedly for work.

One thing White Pine did have in common with others basing their economy on the strength of the silver market, it reeled under the impact when the silver crash came in 1893. Mine owners tried to pretend that things would go on as before. Then one of the best properties, the May-Mazeppa closed down and even the most stout-hearted were forced to admit defeat, with this biggest payroll gone. By 1894 White Pine was deserted, dead.

Then, slowly, life began to flow back. By 1900 some mines were being opened, tentatively. As production increased, the Tomichi Valley smelter, three miles below the town was "blown in", then proceeding to treat 1,000 tons of ore per month. The payroll reached $10,000 a month for a year or two, and optimism soared for a while. But there was not a market for that much silver and things slowed to a halt again. In succeeeding years there were sporadic bursts of activity, interspersed with doldrums. The condition of the camp now would seem permanent, that of death and decay. One or two cabins are sometimes occupied by summer vacationers, though on the occasion of a visit in June of 1964, not a sign of life was to be seen.

TIES ONCE SUPPORTED RAILS which conveyed ore cars from mine tunnel (background) to mill. Several large mills and mines near White Pine now show only wreckage.

OHIO CITY, COLORADO

If friends had not intervened, Reid and Edwards would probably have killed each other in Leadville but in Ohio City, where they had gone separately, they either had no friends or people just loved to see guns blazing and men falling. That was what happened. They saw each other on an Ohio City street in the 1880s. A block apart, their first shots missed, and they continued shooting as they drew closer. When the bullets hit, they were in each others' heart and the men almost touched as they fell.

It was gold that started the excitement at Ohio City, placer gold in the gravels of what would be called Ohio Creek in recognition of the men hailing from that state. The discovery came early in the '60s, making Ohio City one of the oldest camps in the area. When the shallow deposits were exhausted, the men left without searching for the lode that was the natural source. Since the miners had put up only the flimsiest of tents and shacks, all signs of habitation soon disappeared, the small camp slipping back into the wilderness.

Then the big silver boom of 1879 again brought prospectors to Ohio City where they soon found good enough veins to start the camp going again, and more permanently, giving the place the name

LOG CONSTRUCTION of two-story building in Ohio City dates it from silver boom days, before lumber from neighboring Pitkin was available from sawmill there. Corrugated sheet metal roof has saved structure from decay while adjoining dirt-roofed shed is near collapse. Trees on flat in background are cottonwoods bordering Gold Creek, those covering hillside almost all aspens.

ASPENS, the most common and beloved deciduous tree in Colorado's mountain areas, belong to willow family which includes poplars and cottonwoods. Technically **Populus Iremuloides**, trees are conspicuous at all times. Leaves have flat leaf-joints, flutter in slightest breeze showing lighter colored undersides. In Fall, foliage turns brilliant gold, some leaves attaining deeper orange. Heavy massing of trees cause whole mountain sides to blaze with color. Snowy trunks, marked by black "eyes," scars left by self-pruned limbs, are attractive at all times.

of Eagle City, then Ohio City. When the boom collapsed in 1893, Ohio City also caved in, becoming a near-ghost town along with other Colorado silver camps. Then in 1896 a party of prospectors found the vein of gold that had been spilling nuggets into the creek, which they now called Gold Creek.

Ohio City's silver-fostered boom spawned some log buildings but with the gold boom the town of Pitkin up canyon was well established and included a sawmill. So the buildings put up in the gold era are dated by whether they are of logs or lumber.

Muriel Sibell Wolle, in her definitive STAMPEDE TO TIMBERLINE, reports the Carter Group of claims on Gold Creek produced enough ore to keep the twenty-stamp mill going full blast for twenty years, producing a gold brick worth $3,000 every two weeks.

Then there was the Raymond mine which produced steadily until its closure at the death of the manager in 1916. About a mile farther up the gulch were the workings of the Gold Link Mining Company. This outfit had drawn on 6000 acres of gold-bearing claims, operated a forty-stamp mill and kept two hundred men on the payroll. Its main 4000-foot tunnel and many ramifications produced almost a million dollars in gold and silver ore.

PARADISE VALLEY, NEVADA

If Lieut. John Lafferty agreed with scouts who said the only good Indian was a dead one, he had a sound right to his opinion. He spent so much time chasing live Shoshones and Paiutes off settlers' ranches in Paradise Valley, and counting the dead ones, he had little time to go fishing.

And when he did he still had Indian trouble. There was the time in August, 1867, when he went fishing up Cottonwood Creek with Hon. J. A. Banks and Rev. Temple of New York. Banks was a delegate to the Nevada State Constitutional Convention and Speaker of the House at the second legislature. From these labors he took a vacation trip to the fine fishing streams flowing into Paradise Valley from the Santa Rosa Range. Lt. Lafferty, com-

mander of Fort Scott nearby, agreed to go with Banks and the minister.

The three found good fishing but Banks wanted it better. He went on up the creek saying he would return when he had all the trout he wanted. When he failed to return, the lieutenant and Rev. Temple went after him and found his mutilated body in a gully. Lt. Lafferty was enraged, swore vengeance on all Indians and took a party of soldiers after them. They killed several but did not find the murderers of Hon. J. A. Banks.

This was only one incidence in the almost continual strife between whites and Indians in the early days of the town of Paradise Valley. It lay in the grassy, fertile area partly encircled by the Santa

PICTURESQUE BUILDINGS on main street of Paradise Valley. Sun has emerged after hard downpour, fails to reach north—facing side. Structures are among few in West to retain genuine, unspoiled atmosphere of early days. At left is post office established after first was destroyed in fire; next to it tiny shop, meat market at one time—bacon, when available, $1 a pound; next, gambling hall with rooms for girls upstairs, becoming more respectable rooming house later; next, notorious Mecca Saloon, whiskey at 50c a shot, "less for regular customers." Sign is partly discernible behind tree branches.

Rosas. Called Yamoposo by the Indians for its half-moon shape, it earned its English name when in 1863 prospector W. H. Huff climbed to a pass near the top of Santa Rosa Peak, looked out over the land below and exclaimed: "What a Paradise!"

One of Huff's companions was W. C. Gregg. More farmer than miner, the verdant valley so impressed him agriculturally that he brought in a herd of cattle and machinery for cutting and baling hay, thereby setting the pattern for Paradise Valley's future in spite of the hordes of hungry prospectors and miners who swarmed the Santa Rosas over the ensuing years. While some miners did settle in Paradise Valley, and many bought their outfits and provisions there, the real mining towns were Queen City, Spring City, Hardscrabble and the rough and tough Gouge Eye. Spring City was twelve miles away, a typical mining camp spawned in the boom days of the Santa Rosas and boasting of a brewery, seven saloons and a book store.

Gregg, for whom the green of grass was brighter than the glimmer of gold, drew other farmers into the valley. The Santa Rosas handsomely rewarded many with gold but many claims proved shallow or entirely sterile and many miners stayed to grow

hay for the nearby camps, to be used as fodder for riding and work horses.

Richard Bentley and Charles A. Nichols plowed the first furrows for the planting of wheat in the spring of 1864. The settlers put up sod houses and shacks of willow brush, planted large vegetable gardens and cut down the nut pine trees for fuel. And the original inhabitants — Paiutes, Shoshones and Bannocks — watched from the hills. They saw the pastures where game had fed being plowed up and saw the burning of trees which had borne one of their major food supplies, the pine nuts. They watched the sparkling clear streams being dammed, diverted and muddied in sluices and other mining operations.

Then they struck. Small forays grew to mass raids in depredations that lasted for years. The first was an attack on three prospectors just north of the town of Paradise Valley. Dr. H. Smeathman, W. F. White and Frank Thompson were riding out of town when an Indian bullet knocked the doctor off his horse. The other two ignored his cries for help, spurred their mounts on to Rabbit Hole and safety. About two months later a party of four was ambushed near the Santa Rosas, G. W. Dodge slain

STORE AND ORIGINAL POST OFFICE were housed in this structure built around 1870, store established by Charles Kemler, first man to freight supplies into Paradise Valley. Upper floor was dance hall, later boasted hardwood floor mounted on springs, novelty in this sparsely settled section of Nevada. Structure burned in spectacular fire of 1919.

and another man wounded. The next spring, in 1865, Paiute Chief Black Rock Tom organized his tribesmen against the whites, the first casualty being Lucius Arcularius, station keeper on one road and two other whites at another way station. Then came reports the Indians were gathering a war party on the Humboldt. W. H. Haviland of Paradise Valley went to Star City, a thriving mining camp north of Unionville, to ask for help to protect his town from expected attacks.

About the same time two friendly Indians arrived at Aaron Denio's cabin on Martin Creek to warn against an attack intended to slaughter every inhabitant and drive away all stock. Denio spread the alarm and organized plans for complete evacuation.

The fleeing families attempted to reach Willow Point down the Little Humboldt but had difficulty getting their heavily loaded wagons across Cottonwood and Martin Creeks which were running to the banks in spring freshets. Some got the ox-drawn wagons to Hamblin's corral but several stragglers were forced to spend the night in a wayside cabin and awoke to find it surrounded by a party of twenty-two Indians. By a ruse they succeeded in getting away, joining the others at the corral. Then short-

ly this refuge was under attack, the mounted Indians circling and yelling.

The besieged group consisted of ten men, one of whom was Aaron Denio, his 12-year old son Robert, three women and four children. They were armed with three rifles, a musket, two double-barreled shotguns and six revolvers. Everyone seemed agreed that Denio was in command and also that someone would have to go for help.

Whether young Thomas Byrnes was selected or volunteered, there is no doubt of his heroism. He managed to get to the barn without being hit, mounted the fastest horse and headed straight through the lines of screeching Paiutes. Possibly the element of surprise had something to do with the feat but the boy got through, even evading the braves who pursued him, firing as they rode. Thompson and West in their HISTORY OF NEVADA recorded: "It was a race for life. If overtaken by a stray bullet, or the mounted savages, all the lives at the corral would have paid the penalty, and seemingly inspired with the terrible emergency, the noble animal flew like a winged Pegasus out of sight from his pursuers."

The youth must almost have flown as he reached Willow Point at three that afternoon, finding thir-

111

teen men ready and anxious to help. There were only twelve horses and the oldest man named Givens was to be left behind. But as the party started, Givens grabbed one of the saddle pommels and according to the referred to HISTORY: ". . . kept pace with the relief party over the thirteen miles . . . every so often shouting "Heave ahead, boys, heave ahead! The women and children must be saved!', and this while carrying a rifle in his free hand."

The beleaguered group at Hamblin's corral was rescued without a shot being fired. It was just before dark when the Willow Creek party arrived, Given still hanging on. Not sure just how many men comprised the rescuers, the Indians fled. Settlers and deliverers headed for Willow Creek and safety, arriving at three a.m. to find Lt. Joseph Wolverton with a troop of twenty-five men who had responded to Haviland's plea at Star City. Under their protection the Paradise Valley settlers returned to their homes, resuming work in the fields under armed guards.

These and many other Indian incidents resulted in the establishment of two forts in the area — Fort McDermitt at the Oregon border and Fort Winfield Scott a short distance from Paradise Valley. Sporadic Indian fighting continued, with incidents like the fishing party murder of J. A. Banks. It was not until after the winter of 1869 that Indian attacks ceased and Paradise Valley farmers could till their fields without fear.

The protective influence of Fort Winfield Scott encouraged the development of farms and the group of buildings near the fort increased, was in 1866 officially known as Paradise Valley. Charles Kemler who freighted goods into the valley built and operated a store here with a hotel in connection.

The winter of 1867-68 was unusually cold far into spring. Supplies failed to come in and settlers were forced to live on wheat ground in coffee grinders. The next summer A. C. Adams erected his Silver State Flour Mill, putting an end to this. The following year saw the end of the Indian trouble and the start of long, peaceful progress of the agricultural area.

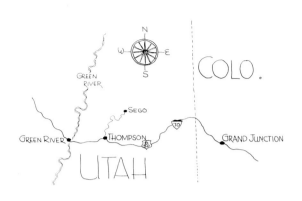

SEGO, UTAH

Coal had none of the glittering lure the fortune hunters found in gold or in the shining veins of silver. There was no glamor or romance in digging out the dull black stuff that lay in sullen defiance of the miner's pick. Yet above ground coal cast the same spell over men that precious metals did, by using the power of the dollar. In camps like Sego they drank and whored and gambled and murdered. As Walter Ronzio says, they worked close to danger and lived right on the edge of it.

Vast areas in western Utah are stark desert, made up of land more or less level relieved by sections where red rock cliffs predominate. Barrenly picturesque, the country has no water except for the Colorado River that bisects the southeastern part of the state. So it was natural enough for one pioneer named Thompson to settle where he found a generous stream of water, about 45 miles from the Colorado state line and 20 from the river. Although this water source was several miles up a narrow canyon, the small settlement growing up around the homestead was called Thompson's Springs.

In the early 1890's the community was made up of farmers, sheepherders and cattlemen, none of whom had ambitions beyond their immediate needs — except Harry Ballard, of England, a man of far-reaching ideas. In a short time he acquired an extensive spread of sheep and cattle and owned most of the village — hotel, store, pool hall and a few houses, enough to cause the Denver and Rio Grande Western Railroad to stop there and build a small station, calling it simply Thompson's. In time the " 's" went too.

Ballard left his herds and flocks to his help and

in roving the country on horseback, made an important discovery about five miles up the canyon near his source of water. Here was a large vein of coal, the seam exposed for yards along the canyon side. Saying nothing of his discovery, he bought up the surrounding land and started mining in a small way.

The coal was first dug by hand and hauled down the narrow canyon by wagon until local customers' wagons came from towns as far away as Monticello and even Bluff, down near the Four Corners. The fame of Ballard's high quality coal spread to Salt Lake City and to B. F. Bauer who owned the Salt Lake Hardware store. Bauer bought out Harry Ballard and formed a corporation, selling stock valued at $1 million. The new company was named American Fuel Co. and the little town around the mines Neslin, after Dick Neslin, new general manager.

Production started in 1911 with ambitious plans, the company erecting a stone store, boarding house and other buildings, all with individual water systems. A coal washer was also constructed, the first west of the Mississippi, and a modern tipple, an elaborate apparatus for emptying coal cars by tipping them.

In 1914 the Denver and Rio Grande Western Railroad built a spur line from Thompson to the coal camp, originally named for Ballard, calling the new line the Ballard and Thompson. In the five-mile stretch the rails crossed the stream thirteen times.

The troubles that plagued the town and mine from beginning to end started with the gradual drying up of the once ample water supply. The level of the water table had been dropping for years but

CENTER OF SEGO, Utah, once busy, rowdy mining camp. At right is company store, walls of sturdy rock still standing though with numerous cracks, ceilings, floors and partitions long gone. At left is boarding house. Few hundred feet below these structures are two others in fairly good condition but rest are in partial or complete ruin. Shown here is one of thirteen bridges once spanning dry gulch which contained lively stream in early days. Bridges, originally built to carry railroad spur, later road, are to be crossed with caution, taking care to keep wheels on lengthwise planks.

was ignored until one summer the spring dried to a dribble, not enough to operate the coal washer. The little "600" steam engine operated by the D. & R.G.W. which pulled four cars of coal to and from the tipple was off the track one fourth of the time or would often go careening down the tracks out of control.

Discouraged with a program yielding little or no profit, majority stockholder Bauer insisted on a general reorganization in 1916. Among officers who got the boot was Dick Neslin, and with his banishment the town became Sego, the Mormon name for *Calochortus Nuttalli*, state flower of Utah. He was replaced by a Mr. Van Dirck and the operation to be known as Chesterfield Coal Co.

Walter Ronzio, now of Grand Junction, Colorado, was only fourteen years old when he went to work in the Sego coal mines. July 18, 1918. He describes some of the financial troubles of the Chesterfield people and their employees:

"The reorganization didn't help much as far as the miners were concerned. Pay days would lag behind sometimes as long as a year. The mine owners would announce a pay day and we would all line up at the pay window. We were supposed to get a month or two of the six or seven months owing. Maybe a third of the line would receive their pay. Then the clerk would say, 'Sorry, no more money'. However no one actually lost any money. To those who didn't get paid the company would issue scrip

114

money. With this you could buy supplies in the company store, gamble or spend it for white mule or home brew. If you needed a little cash maybe you could find some one who would give you $3 cash for say $5 worth of scrip.

"Those were days when it didn't make any difference how provoked you got at the management, you just kept your mouth shut or the boss would say—You're fired! The only thing we could do as American citizens was to quit. But most of us had families that were at least eating." However continuing dissatisfaction at last caused the men to welcome previously rejected organizers of the United Mine Workers Union. Unionization was accomplished in 1933 after which miners were paid regularly twice a month.

Up until 1927 the company supplied its own power for mine operation and electricity for the camp, using a pair of Lance engines which were a constant headache, frequently breaking down. The company knew that if mining were to continue power would have to be secured from some other source. The nearest available electricity was at Columbia, Utah, a hundred miles away, but a line was built by Chesterfield, carrying 44,000 volts, at a cost of more than $100,000, the company forced to guarantee twenty years' use. The first power arrived in Sego November 1, 1927, and exactly twenty years later to the day, the Chesterfield mines were ordered closed, property offered at a sheriff's sale on the courthouse steps at Moab, Utah.

By then the one-time total of 125 miners employed had dwindled to 27. Among them was Walter Ronzio. He had spent almost 30 years working

DESOLATION AND RUIN prevail in Sego. At left is rear of company store where miner could spend scrip, received from mine when payroll was short. At right is one of two "American" boarding houses. Strict segregation of races prevailed in living, if not working quarters. Greek miners had own boarding house as did Japanese, Negroes living in group of shacks in another section. Steady dropping of water table was first evident when vegetable gardens dried up and water supply became inadequate for coal washers. Trees here managed sizeable growth before dying.

DOZENS OF PRIMITIVE DWELLINGS line sides of canyon at Sego. Once home for miner and family, this dug-out now collects tumbleweeds and roof beams rot away. Most of "house" was scooped out of bank, rocks removed used to fashion front wall. Place lacked windows, water and plumbing but in later years had electricity.

in the mines. They were his life. His father went to work there in 1913, the family taking up a homestead about a mile down the canyon and living temporarily at Green River, Utah. With the father well established in his mine job, he moved his wife and two boys to the homestead, their first shelter an open cave in the cliff side, its roof a ledge protruding from the vertical wall. The children were fascinated by the many Indian petroglyphs engraved on the surrounding red rock walls, a veritable picture gallery. For more comfortable quarters the father set up two tents, dug a well and then built a house of native rock. The ruins still stand about a quarter mile above the point where the railroad is cut through solid rock.

Father and sons raised 60 tons of hay a year and planted a large vegetable garden, selling carrots, cabbages and greens in the camp. During those first years there was plenty of water available for irrigation and all crops raised in the comparatively short season flourished. The Ronzio family literally had its roots in the canyon and the mines.

OLD MINE TUNNEL follows vein of coal shown at left in one of earliest operations, possibly that of original owner, Harry Ballard.

PLUMBING, sanitary facilities in Sego were of the simplest and most "johns" were decorated with familiar star and crescent. Yards contain many dead or dying apricot trees, generous producers in day of more plentiful water supply.

RELIC from old-time kitchen when Sego's coal mines furnished its heat and livelihood for as many as 125 miners, some with families. View looks toward mouth of canyon which widens out here. Most of town was confined between narrow, rocky walls.

The announcement of the closing and impending sale of the mine plant was a staggering blow to Walter and the other men. He called a meeting to discuss what might be done to save the situation. They decided to attempt purchase at the auction, each man to account for an equal number of shares — 1200 at a dollar a share. Not every man had the cash but those lacking it promised to pay what was owing through future payroll deductions. The total cash raised was $18,000 and two banks offered to loan the group the remaining up to $30,000. At the auction the bidding got up to that figure and Walter Ronzio topped it by $10. The entire operation — camp, buildings, equipment and all assets — passed into the hands of the miners for $30,010 and they wisely insisted on a clause giving them mineral rights to all land involved. They formed a corporation under the name of the Utah Grand Coal Co. and elected Walter Ronzio as general manager.

Within a year the Utah Grand Coal Co. was on its feet with all obligations paid. Then, as Walter relates, "things began to happen." The first catastrophe was the July 1, 1949, destruction by fire of the tipple, origin of the blaze never determined. This curtailed production drastically and the railroad notified Ronzio it could no longer profitably operate the spur to Sego. The company, it said, could build ramps for truck loading and haul the coal down to Thompson where the railroad would be glad to pick it up. This meant building a new tipple, purchasing two dump trucks and a boxcar loader. The men made the hard decision to go ahead, closing down for five months for changes and equipment installation. Work started in the middle of December with a general feeling of great optimism but calamity had more evil work to do. In two weeks another disastrous fire struck, starting in the lamp-changing rack, and completely destroying the shops. All spare machine parts were lost as was repair equipment. Any breakdown now meant closure.

Recovery was slow but persistent, the biggest

ONE LARGER HOUSE was built out of whatever came to hand, taking advantage of huge rock to form one wall. Roof is of beams covered with earth which grows scant crop of grass. Flat surfaces in many red rock cliffs were used by vanished Indian tribes as art galleries, larger surfaces for paintings, petroglyphs of heroic proportions showing tribal chiefs with hour-glass figures and triangular heads. Among other paleontological specimens found in mines by Chesterfield Co. were huge dinosaur tracks, one measuring 44x32 inches. Some tracks indicated reptilian stride of 15 feet and animal height of 35 feet.

aid being the stockpile of big lump coal. Readily handled and loaded in boxcars it was rail shipped to mid-west points. The smaller nut and sack coal produced by screening was used by the railroad, sales of this covering the cost of producing the larger sizes. But again came a blow, the fatal one. The railroad changed over to the new diesel fuel for its locomotives. The doom of the coal mines was sealed.

In February of 1955, the Utah Grand sold its holdings to Seaburg Brothers of Dayton, Texas. The amount paid, $25,000, was not for the valueless coal mines but for 700 acres of land with mineral rights. Tests showed both oil and natural gas in the formation including the site of Sego.

Long before this Walter's brother and father had passed away. In February of 1960 he and his mother sold the old homestead in the canyon to a group of sheepmen from Glenwood, Colorado, and moved to Grand Junction. There he operates a hotel-apartment house, his mother at 86 residing with him.

Now, ten years after the sale of the townsite, Sego is a very dead ghost but not a cold one. At least one large vein of coal is burning, the ground hot and crusty, very unsafe to walk on. Several vents, one two feet across which shoots a column of steam and smoke, produce the only tangible wraiths in our experience.

FRONT OF COMPANY STORE, interior now empty cavern floored by basement ceiling. Cottonwood tree hangs precariously to life, obviously reaching sub-moisture denied others on slightly higher ground behind building.

RED ROCK FORMATIONS at Sego, called "Book Cliffs" because of many petroglyphs contained extend southward to culminate at near-by Arches National Monument. Among many spectacular sand - carved shapes is "Delicate Arch", called by early cowboys "The Schoolmarm's Pants." Arches and other fantastic forms are eroded through several strata of sandstone, Navajo, Carmel and Entrada. Each displays different tones of red, buff and salmon pink.

FOLSOM, NEW MEXICO

It cost Madison Emery a cow to keep peace with the Indians camped just outside the village. He was trying to explain that neither he nor his stepson had anything to do with the dead buck when there was a sudden rattle-bang of explosions and the peace pipe went out. The "shots" were found to be only rifle cartridges in the stove but the situation was touchy, and well — what was a cow if the Indians would go away?

The town of Folsom, named for President Cleveland's wife Frances Folsom, began as a tiny hamlet close to the present town. Called Madison for the first settler, Madison Emery, the site has disappeared so completely none of Folsom's residents ever heard of it.

When Emery arrived on the scene in 1862 he found the grass in the valley so tall it would hide a man on a horse, the hills covered with a fine stand of pinon pines, streams filled with fish and game abundant. He built a cabin and as more families made homes, stores and other businesses sprang up, he erected a rough hotel.

The frontier town was constantly harassed by Indians and was especially apprehensive when they made semi-permanent camps near the village. On one of those occasions Bud Sumpter, Emery's stepson, found an Indian lying behind the store. He thought the brave was asleep until he turned him over, but he was dead apparently from too much firewater.

Emery feared violence from the Indians who might doubt the manner of the buck's death, invited the chief and council to his home for a parley. Progress was being made when there was a furious fusillade of what seemed to be gunshots and all those present dived for doors and windows. When it was discovered the "shots" were cartridges some prankster had dropped in the kitchen stove, the redmen were persuaded to return and relight the peace pipe. Harmony seemed assured when Emery presented the chief with his fattest cow.

Madison was the nearest settlement to the "Robbers' Roost" just north of Kenton in neighboring Oklahoma. Periodically the notorious Coe and his gang would make a hurried visit to Madison when they scented a raid on the hideout. They would pull up in front of the inn run by Mrs. Emery, order the horses "serviced" at gun point, then repair to the nearest saloon. After tanking up, the outlaws would demand a meal from Mrs. Emery, sleep off food and drink in her beds and sweep away at dawn like so many scavenger crows. Then everybody in Madison breathed easier.

Coe's outlawry got important enough to set the U.S. Cavalry after him. A company from Fort Lyons, Colorado, moved into Kenton, flushed the gang and Coe slipped over to his safe refuge at the Emerys. This time it was not so safe. A detachment from Fort Union, New Mexico, was bivouacked behind a hill. Mrs. Emery fed and wined the bandit and as soon as he was asleep, sent her son Bud on his pony to alert the soldiers. He returned with a guard which arrested Coe. As the badman was led from the house he remarked: "That pony has had

FOLSOM HOTEL operated recently enough to provide T.V. for guests, was in 1964 completely abandoned. Below stoutly built structure is solid block of similar stone buildings, all empty except grocery.

a hard ride". To avoid reprisals on the Emerys, Coe was taken to Pueblo, Colorado, to await trial. It never came, his widespread fame proving his undoing. A Vigilante Committee broke into the calaboose at night, snatched the bandit and strung him up, leg irons and all. The mystery of his disappearance from jail remained for years until someone found his skeleton, hardware still attached.

But what lawlessness could not do to Madison, the coming of the Colorado and Southern Railroad did. Because the line bypassed the town just enough to cause it to seek a new site, the original town languished and utterly vanished. At the new location shelters and business establishments were all tents, giving the clutter the name of "Ragtown", but it got a new one — Folsom — when it developed quickly. The rails came in 1887-1888 and by 1895 Folsom had two mercantile stores, three saloons and several other businesses including two houses which were not homes. One reason for the rapid growth was, being on the railroad it had the largest stockyards north of Fort Worth.

But the change in the town was not to the credit of law and order. The first citizen of Folsom was

W. A. Thompson, proprietor of the Gem Saloon and deputy sheriff. He came from Missouri under a cloud, charged with the murder of a man and in Folsom racked up a record as lurid as that of any other New Mexico badman, in a state that produced Bill the Kid, Clay Allison and others of that ilk.

One time he shot point blank at an erstwhile friend, killing him and gave as the reason: "The dirty so-and-so had the nerve to get drunk in another saloon." Again, infuriated at a taunt from a local lad in his saloon, he pursued the boy outdoors, firing as he ran. One of the bullets went through the stove of a neighbor but all missed the boy, who escaped. Raging inwardly, Thompson turned his gun on anyone within range including Bill Thatcher, a fellow officer but bitter enemy, and Jeff Kiel who had emerged from King's Store. Thatcher was wounded seriously and Kiel fatally. Thatcher managed to shoot Thompson's gun from his hands, the crazed assailant running into his saloon and barricading the doors.

A crowd bent on lynching quickly gathered outside but short of burning the building and endangering the entire block, they could not get

122

Thompson out. When waiting cooled the mob's temper, Thompson staggered forth dead drunk and collapsed. Authorities took him to the Clayton jail, then to Springer.

Released on bond, he returned to Folsom, sold his saloon and cleared up all personal matters. At the murder trial in Clayton he was acquitted, a verdict that would have been impossible nearer home. He then moved to Trinidad and married the girl for whom he had committed his first murder. The couple later went to Oklahoma where Thompson killed another person and was again acquitted.

In 1908 the town had that new-fangled contraption, the telephone, switchboard being in the home of Sarah J. Rooke on the edge of town. One night in August Sarah answered her buzzer to hear a voice shout that a huge wave from a flash flood was racing down the river and would strike the town in minutes, warning to get people out of town without trying to rescue any possessions. Sarah was too busy to go, but rang one bell after another, as many as she could before the water hit. Her own house was swept from its foundations, girl and switchboard with it. Her body was found eight miles below the town. Most buildings had been carried away and seventeen persons drowned, yet many were saved because of Sarah's heroism. Grateful citizens of Folsom and other nearby towns contributed funds for a granite memorial at her grave.

But Folsom's most prominent citizen was the "Folsom Man", existing only by deduction. Archeologists had long been interested in an arroyo close to the town where they had found superficial evidences of artifacts dating from the Pleistocene or Ice Age, some 20,000 years ago. In 1927 more careful digging revealed a cache of bones belonging to ice age animals, most of them slain by man-made weapons such as exquisitely fashioned lances or

MOST BUILDINGS in Folsom are constructed of stone, have well withstood ravages of time. Water tower, windmill were supported on top of log tripod at left. Folsom is geologically fascinating as Capulin National Monument. Area contains nine small near-perfect craters in addition to Mount Capulin, 8368 feet. Main cinder cone, of recent formation, is one mile in diameter at base, 1450 feet at summit, is considered most nearly symmetrical volcano in this country.

BUSY ESTABLISHMENT during heyday of Folsom. Building sheltered Doherty Investment Co., general store, market and early post office. Present one is housed in its own small building, faces imminent closure.

spear points, some found among the bones. In several instances a point was imbedded in a bone. Made of flint, they showed careful workmanship, finely fluted along the edges.

Although no human remains were found, the discovery dated the existence of man in North America much earlier than previously estimated, 1000 B.C. It has since been substantiated that these first settlers of Folsom were descendants of wanderers who crossed from Asia over a land bridge, moving on to New Mexico. Although most of the northern lands were still covered by deep ice deposits, there was a corridor of bare ground parallel to the east side of the Rocky Mountains along which men and animals could migrate. Later similar discoveries near the Sandia Mountains, also in New Mexico, suggested an even earlier date for the presence of these immigrants.

WIDE OPEN SPACES, typical of country between Folsom and Cimarron—vast, lonely, awe-inspiring.

WATROUS, NEW MEXICO

Soldiering "Out West" was all right, except for the twenty-four hour leaves. Most of the time all you had to do was see you didn't sleep next to a rattlesnake or let some Apache get close enough to put a hole in your ear. It was those floozies in town that put your foot in the gopher hole.

Soldiers on leave from old Fort Union were offered a choice in places for hell raising. Las Vegas had more kinds of bordellos but it was twenty miles farther than Watrous. The correspondent in that town contributed this item in the Las Vegas OPTIC of November 28.

"One of the soldier boys from Fort Union came to our town to have the pleasures of gambling his money at our saloons. After four or five hours he came out without much success, and insisted on our citizens to loan him money, which they did, and after having success on borrowed money failed to divide up, after which harsh words ensued between parties and causing our soldier to receive one eye loss. Our doctor claims the eye is ruined. We feel sorry for his losing his eye, and also his money. Would not consider it a safe and pleasant place for boys to come and spend their money."

When the boys wore out their welcome in Watrous, they turned to even smaller Loma Parda which soon got tired of roistering soldiers, boarded up all business places and closed up. Then back to Watrous went the soldiers and back in the news they came, just after Christmas. "On Christmas Day," wrote the OPTIC correspondent, "there was horse racing at Watrous as well as at Tiptonville. The school children went from Watrous to Tiptonville (where the Mission school was located) to sing Christmas carols. All was quiet until the body of a soldier from Fort Union was found in the Mora

TWO WELLS about six feet apart showing water table was near surface and well digging easy. Watrous was built on point of land at junction of Mora and Sapello Rivers, first settlement called La Juncta de los Rios. Well nearest camera served cabin behind photographer, house shown one of group built in earliest days of town, all fashioned of logs, brush, anything available, then covered with thick layer of "stucco"—hard-setting native clay.

River. Since the excitement caused by the visit of four drunken soldiers and the finding of the dead body of one of them in the Mora River a few days afterwards, nothing has happened to disturb the quietness of our town until last Sunday. On that day a rumor reached us that soldiers from Fort Union were coming to raid our town in revenge for their comrades. But they didn't come which was fortunate for them as our citizens were prepared for anything of the kind and any visitors on any such errand will meet with a hearty reception, and find they have not got another Loma Parda to deal with. It is but justice to state that the better class of soldiers at the fort, together with the officers, condemn any such demonstrations, and the perpetrators of the last outrages will be severely dealt with."

In the early days Watrous was known to Indians and Mexicans as La Juncta de los Rios, the name describing the location of the village at the junction of the Mora and Sapello Rivers. Originally a meeting and barter place for pueblo and plains Indians, it became the gathering area for sheep herders from Las Vegas, Mora, Abiquiu, La Questa, Antonchico, Albuquerque and Manzano. Nearby were camps of transient comancheros, Comanches, Utes, Kiowas, Cheyennes, Arapahoes, Navajos and Apaches.

By 1801 the spot was where mule trains of all sorts stopped, most of them carrying cargo valuable in a land where comforts of civilization were few. They attracted bandits who could sell stolen tobacco, jewelry, furs and other luxury items. Yet in spite of constant depredations, the beauty of the locality with ample water supply and extensive green pastures for stock was so appealing many merchants — drivers tarried and even settled down to stay.

New Mexico was still under Spanish control for not until 1821 did it become independent, then a province of Mexico and in 1848 a part of the United States. It was the age of land grants and Governor Armijo was known to be generous in bestowing vast acreages upon prospective settlers. At Juncta de los Rios a group of farmers banded together, drawing up a formal petition to Armijo for the surrounding lands. While legalities were pending, raids by

STONE HOUSE, walls covered with clay mud, then finished with finer clay and painted. Long unused, building served many purposes — saloon, dance hall, store. During '80s it was remodeled for livery stable, blacksmith shop. Many other original buildings remain in Watrous.

marauding Jicarilla Apaches discouraged some petitioners but the steadfast were eventually rewarded with deeds to the property.

When Samuel B. Watrous arrived on the scene he was footloose and fancy free, not interested in land grants. When he did decide to settle down he was too late for the free land deal and was forced to buy his farm from one of the original grantees. Born in Connecticut, orphaned at an early age, Sam was sent to live with an uncle in Vermont. The boy resented what he thought was undue discipline imposed by the uncle together with very early rising, before breakfast chores and day long hard labor. He fled, joined a wagon train heading west, arrived in Taos, New Mexico, to work as clerk in a store. Young Sam quickly caught the popular fever and headed up the Rio Grande with a gold pan at every chance. The virus hung on and he gave up the clerking job for the booming placer mines of San Pedro. The good ground was all taken and finally discouraged with mining, he married and went back to storekeeping, this time on his own, in the village of San Norios.

In a few years he fell ill and forced outdoors by doctor's warnings, he left wife Josephine to run the store and took off for the hills. He spent much time with various Indian tribes and acquired knowledge of their ways which was to prove valuable in later years of frequent clashes with raiding Apaches.

Now the wanderer made up his mind to earn his living on a farm and cast his eye on part of the parcel called La Juncta de los Rios. After years of legal delay, title was finally cleared and in May, 1846, Sam Watrous bought out Richard Dallam's interest in the grant. Josephine joined her husband, the farm and business affairs of Samuel Watrous flourished and he became a leading member of the community.

One of the larger enterprises was the general mercantile, operated by partners Watrous, Thomas Rice and Sam's son-in-law, William Tipton. This was broken up in 1865, Sam's son Joseph becoming the new partner, the store operating as S. B. Watrous & Son. It was about this time the Watrous herds and flocks pastured near Tucumcari were being repeatedly run off by Comanches and Kiowas, Watrous' locally good relations with Indians apparently not extending to that area.

Then in 1879 came news that the Santa Fe Railroad would build through La Juncta de los Rios and public spirited Sam and son promptly donated land for right-of-way, station and yards.

But Sam was most surprised of all to see WATROUS on the new depot's name board. Officials told him it was the least they could do and moreover there was already one station named La Juncta de los Rios in Colorado.

S. B. Watrous & Son also donated land for a park, fenced it, planted trees, all providing if and when the county seat came to Watrous, the courthouse would be erected on it. When neighboring Mora got the prize the Watrous interests did not sulk but set about getting a fine new school house, donating land and initiating a campaign for building funds. At first the project seemed to be a success but it fell through when pledged money failed to materialize. The disappointment to Watrous was all the more bitter because the upstart neighbor Tipton, which did get the school, was founded by son-in-law William Tipton, Sam's ex-partner.

There might have been biological reasons for the school going to Tipton. Its founder also started a population explosion sufficient to fill it. A roster of pupils in 1881 shows two Watrous descendants, Charles and Rose, followed by Lizzie Tipton, Susan Tipton, Martin Tipton, Louise Tipton, W. B. Tipton, Tom Tipton, Charles Tipton, Ella Tipton and several less numerous representatives of other pioneer families.

Another newspaper item, this one dated February, 1888, shows that life at Watrous and environs continued to be as interesting as in earlier days. "James Lafer, who was arrested at Watrous, was wanted for a murder he committed in Olean, New York in 1882, for which his twin brother served two years imprisonment but was pardoned when he turned out to be the wrong man. This Lafer was run out of Las Vegas as a bad character. He worked as a cowboy and was known as a rustler. He would shoot on the slightest provocation. On more than one occasion he cleaned out the town of Watrous, riding in and terrorizing the people by firing revolvers promiscuously through the streets. He once rode into Fort Union in the middle of the night and tried to assault the sentry who was walking post but was captured and slightly wounded in the melee. In Loma Parda he is still remembered as the man who picked up a New Mexican woman in the street, placed her across the horse in front of him, and rode into the saloon, making the bartender set up drinks for the whole party, and because his horse would not drink, he shot him through the head, lifted the woman from the saddle before the horse fell, and walked out, leaving the horse dead on the floor."

THIS SECTION of old two-story stone building proved Watrous was not a "one horse" town, that country had many. Interior is equipped with huge forge, many anvils. Plows were made and repaired here, farm equipment kept in condition, horses shod and harness made usable.

129

CHRONIC DIFFICULTY holding back full development of milling rich ore from mines in high country near Cimarron was lack of consistent water power. Invention of new "impulse type" of water wheel by Lester Allen Pelton in Camptonville, Calif., 1878 was hailed as answer to problem, since wheel required only small volume of water for operation. Although much of metals mining boom in northern New Mexico was already finished by then, some Pelton wheels were imported, proved to be only another disappointment. Though jet of water could be small it had to be directed at cups with great velocity not obtainable at all times.

CIMARRON, NEW MEXICO

"A house is not a home", said a certain madam of distinction, but it is possible to have a home with a house in it. Cimarron land owner Lucien B. Maxwell had one. The mammoth house, as large as a city block, was essentially a hotel containing quarters for Maxwell when he was not riding over his vast domain, as well as gambling rooms, saloon, dance hall, billiard parlor. Then there was the special area reserved for women of special virtue — and they were permanent fixtures. Once a girl was installed in these lavishly furnished rooms she was allowed to leave only if she were not coming back.

The Maxwell estate was three times as large as the State of Rhode Island, comprising 1,714,765 acres. Besides Cimarron, the area included the sites of Springer, Raton and Elizabethtown in New Mexico, spreading well over into Colorado to take in Segundo and other towns. French trapper Don Carlos Beaubien and his Spanish or Mexican partner Guadalupe Miranda, applied for a grant in 1841 and used the land as their own although legal title was held up for 41 years. An ex-trapper, hailing from Kaskaskia, Illinois, Maxwell came exploring, joined General Fremont's expedition and married Luz Beaubien, Don Carlos' daughter. In 1849 the couple settled on the Beaubien-Miranda Grant, and upon the father-in-law's death in 1864, bought out the other heirs, becoming the owners of the largest land grant in New Mexico.

Maxwell's family included four daughters and a son Peter, whom the father despised because the boy would not share his interests and "wasted his time with worthless friends." Maxwell did favor one daughter, Virginia, but when she met Captain A. S. B. Keyes, associated in Indian Agency operations, father objected violently to the romance, but finally did give grudging but unforgiving consent to the marriage. The wedding on the top floor of the estate granary was a brilliant social event — but Lucien Maxwell did not attend.

When he first took over the grant, Maxwell lost no time in getting a herd of cattle established and with complete control of it, industriously increased the herds by setting up individual ranchers with their own cattle, tenants to make payments on a share basis. It was typical of the times that no contracts were ever drawn up, all agreements being verbal.

At about 6000 feet in elevation most of the grassy meadows around Cimarron were assured of ample rainfall for good pasturage and Maxwell's herds flourished. He quickly had a surplus to market, the main outlet a scattered group of accessible army posts. He sold only the extra cattle to their commissaries, keeping his best animals and upgrading the remaining stock. And he maintained a diversity in the stock, saddle and work horses grazing in the pastures, more hilly sections supporting flocks of sheep. There was even a large goat ranch, its manager to be well known in later years as Buffalo Bill Cody.

But Maxwell was not content with agrarian

projects. Noting the many prospectors, trappers and travelers along the Santa Fe Trail who were camping just anywhere, he decided to build a huge stopping place for them. It was not a humanitarian gesture to shelter them from rain and snow. This was business. He would provide amusements for these lonely men, liquor to warm their bellies, faro, roulette, monte and female companionship — to divert the flow of gold to Santa Fe.

The Maxwell House was built in 1864 and was soon the center of social life in northern New Mexico, as well as the principal "wayside inn." The old registers contained some prominent names but if a guest chose not to sign for reasons of his own, he was not refused. Davy Crockett — the desperado, not the legendary character of an earlier era — Kit Carson, Clay Allison and Buffalo Bill, who occasionally came in from the lonely post on the goat ranch to live it up a little, were a few of the famous guests. Cody's visits were not all dalliance as it was in Cimarron he organized the first of his Wild West Shows.

There were some shooting scrapes in the Maxwell House, particularly in the bar and gambling sections, but participants were quickly ejected or carried out, Maxwell not tolerating such nonsense as it was bad for business, he said. But bullets flew freely elsewhere in Cimarron. One man who seemed to attract them was burly Mason Chase, red-headed son of a rancher. On one occasion there was a "shivaree" going on at the Cosgrove house. It had started as a celebration for a newly married couple but had gotten out of hand from too much red eye.

Young Charles Cosgrove stepped outside to run off the demonstrators when Mason Chase came along wanting to know what the party was all about. The infuriated Cosgrove, assuming Chase was the instigator, raised his gun and fired point blank at Chase's heart. But the red-head stayed upright. Recently made deputy sheriff, he made notes on his job in a thick notebook carried in his breast pocket and it received the bullet. Later he complained he could not read some of the writing in it.

Not so lucky was bandit Davy Crockett who had the town of Cimarron and countryside under his control. In September of 1876 he met up with Deputy Sheriff Joe Holbrook. It was a case of which man was quicker on the draw and Crockett was buried on Cimarron's boot hill. Friends placed a headboard at his grave but vandals later carried it off as a souvenir.

Clay Allison was another badman who kept the town in a turmoil. Historian Charles Siringo

OLD CIMARRON JAIL has heavy plank door with tiny barred window. From this opening peered long succession of outlaws, murderers, horse thieves, many emerging only for noose around necks.

"credits" him with eighteen victims, the most modest estimates being ten. J. Frank Dobie, beloved western writer who passed away in 1964, said of Allison: "He was quixotically independent in interpreting what constituted his rights. The more whiskey he drank, the more rights he possessed and sometimes when he came to town he bought a great deal of whiskey. He was generous with it, however, even insisting on his horse enjoying a fair portion."

Allison was twenty years old at the start of the Civil War and he joined the Confederate side. Captured by Union soldiers, he was convicted of spying and sentenced to be shot. He was held in a makeshift prison and although six feet two and weighing one hundred and eighty pounds, he had deceptively small hands and was able to slip out of his handcuffs and escape.

Allison liked off-the-trail types of duels when

involved in quarrels. He once got his adversary to stand at one end of a freshly dug grave facing the pit, Allison at the other, winner to cover up the loser. Another was brought on by Allison's killing Pancho Grieg in a flareup over a billiard game in Cimarron's St. James Hotel. He remarked it sure was a hot day and taking off his hat, used it for a fan and with a tricky movement drew his gun under cover of the hat, shooting Pancho dead.

Sheriff Mace Bowman told Allison his actions in the affair were not entirely ethical and suggested the gunman give himself up. Allison had a proposition ready. He and the sheriff would lay their guns on the bar of Lambert's Hotel (officially the St. James). They would stand back to back and at a

given signal, walk twenty-five paces. Then at another signal they would rush for their guns. The sheriff allowed this was a reasonable arrangement, possibly because he knew Allison had accidentally shot himself in the foot not long before and might be handicapped. He figured wrong. Allison won the dash and leveled his gun at the sheriff. Bowman then stood straight, exposed his chest and said: "All right, shoot me, you ....!" But Allison admired such courage and answered: "Mace, you're too brave a man to die," placing his gun back in its holster. The two then shook hands and justice, frontier fashion, was done. Allison's death came some years later in ironical fashion. The gunman was full of whiskey and driving a team of four mules

CENTURY OLD GRANARY and grist mill was built to hold and grind grain produced on Maxwell Grant. It seems as solid today as when built in 1864, all floors solid and safe. This view shows north or rear, facing on nearby Cimarron River. Front side once had ramp affording access to second floor. Wedding of Virginia Maxwell and Capt. A. S. B. Keyes was held here.

when the wagon hit a sharp bump. Allison was bounced out and the wheels of the heavy rig rolled over his head, crushing it "like an eggshell," said the freighter traveling with him.

The Las Vegas GAZETTE took a laconic view of the goings on at Cimarron, reporting once: "Everything is quiet at Cimarron. Nobody has been killed there in three days." The town boasted of fifteen saloons where gunmen could get their courage up, four hotels, a post office and a miniature printing plant where a weekly paper, the Cimarron NEWS AND PRESS, was published. The spindly hand-press was said to have been first used by Padre Antonio Jose Martinez to print his little Taos paper, EL CREPUSCULE. One day the NEWS AND PRESS incautiously hit the street with an editorial blistering some of the gunmen terrorizing the town. That night the ouraged outlaws broke into the newspaper office housed in the Indian Agency headquarters and smashed the press, dumping the wreckage and type cases in the Cimarron River.

The mother of Mason Chase was one of the forthright women in Cimarron. On an autumn day when the leaves were yellowing, the apples in her little orchard ripening, she shook the branches and let the fruit fall into her apron. A wildcat on an upper branch suddenly dropped on the woman, clawing and biting her. After getting her hands on the animal's throat, she squeezed the windpipe until the struggling cat went limp. Then Mrs. Chase calmly gathered the scattered apples into her apron and went home.

And it was Mrs. Chase's daughter-in-law, wife of Mason, who was struck by lightning and lived, although doomed to carry a lifetime reminder of the incident. Hope Gilbert, now of Pasadena, California, who lived in Cimarron as a child, heard the story from Tom McBride, born on the Chase ranch. Before she was married, Nellie Curtis Chase traveled with her family to a dance about five miles from home. She rode on the front seat of an open spring wagon beside the driver and her sister. The sky was ominous when they started and during the rain a flash of lightning made a direct hit on the wagon. The mule pulling it was knocked to the ground and the dog running alongside killed. The driver was stunned and Nellie appeared dead, clothes burned from her body, gold necklace melted and imbedded in the skin. Unconscious for several days, the girl survived but all the rest of her life the mark of the lightning-fused necklace remained around her neck.

Lucien Maxwell stayed with stock raising and

MECHANISM ONCE OPERATING grinding stones, still intact on floor above, was powered by generous water flow diverted from Cimarron River. When Lucien Maxwell was made head of U.S. Government Indian Agency, he dispensed flour and provisions to Utes and Apaches from store in granary. Well educated, six feet tall with fair complexion and blue eyes, friendly "White Father" was highly regarded by Indians who felt protective toward Maxwell ranch, on at least one occasion preventing raid by hostile tribe.

inn keeping, and succeeded mightily. He employed five hundred men on the ranches, several thousand acres of rich land producing hay and other crops. His contracts with the government expanded and money poured into his coffers, which was in truth a cowhide trunk in his bedroom, the rancher having little faith in banks.

In the middle '60s gold was discovered on various streams within the Maxwell Grant boundaries. At first these were kept secret, the discoverers fearing ejection and reprisals from the big boss. But when the news did leak out, he took no action and the three men involved in the earliest workings formed a company — head officers: W. H. Moore,

William Koenig and John Buck. Without opposition the outfit successfully mined its claims.

Then even larger deposits were found by two other partners — Brownson and Kelly — in nearby Moreno Valley, but the tiny stream there failed to supply enough water for washing operations. The finders staked their claims, however, and dreamed of obtaining water by diverting some of the flow of Red River in Taos County. Such a scheme would require a big fund but the men set about organizing a stock company to finance the ditch.

First they approached Maxwell with an offer of stock in the company and the man who had done so well at ranching and cattle raising made his first big mistake. He invested heavily in the venture and as the company began to run out of money long before the ditch was finished, he was approached again for further funds. The project took $300,000 for completion and it is probable Lucien Maxwell supplied most of it.

The NEW MEXICO MINER reported: "It was a colossal undertaking . . . a marvelous piece of engineering. The ditch forms three-fourths of a circle in its length of skirting along the edge of the mountains, bridging ravines and gullies." But the article left out some painful details such as the fact that so many leaks developed along the long canal that little water arrived at the lower end. Although extensive repairs were made with expensive maintenance kept up, it was never a success, but considerable gold was extracted with its aid. Some time later the MINER was forced to modify its opinion, stating: "The Lynch Ditch which carries water from Red River to the Moreno placer mines at Elizabethtown is to be sold next month at a sheriff's sale to satisfy a judgment and cost aggregating $7,000."

From one disastrous debacle, Maxwell turned to another. He started the First National Bank of Santa Fe, charter granted in December, 1870. It took him only a year to discover banking was somewhat more complex than stuffing money into a cowhide trunk and he sold out at a heavy loss. Now he was approached by a group seeking to finance the building of the Texas Pacific Railroad and the man born to raise hay and cattle invested $250,000. When it failed, Maxwell retired to his ranch to lick his wounds. In 1870 he sold his grant, lock-stock-and barrel to a group of financiers for around $750,000 and moved to Fort Sumner, which had been demili-

tarized and offered for sale by the government. Maxwell bought the part having buildings and other improvements, remodeling the officers' quarters into a luxurious home with twenty rooms. Here he lived in semi-retirement until he died in 1875, leaving his property to his son Peter.

Peter Maxwell was described as a "well meaning, inoffensive man, but very timid" by John W. Poe, deputy of Lincoln County sheriff Pat Garrett. On the hot night of July 14, 1881, Peter had given sanctuary to the notorious gunman Billy the Kid, who was on the run after being convicted of murder and sentenced to hang in April at Lincoln. He escaped from jail there, killing two guards as he fled. Garrett and his deputies tracked him to Fort Sumner and the Kid was slain by Garrett in young Maxwell's bedroom. He was buried in the old military cemetery where Lucien B. Maxwell already lay, and where Peter was buried at his death.

Cimarron had its turn, from 1872 to 1882, at being county seat of Colfax, a county credited with having more of them than any other in the country. Elizabethtown was one, others Springer, Raton and even little Colfax almost made it. By 1880, Cimarron was getting somewhat ghostly, becoming a true wraith after removal of the county seat. Twenty-five years later the St. Louis, Rocky Mountain and Pacific Railroad built a spur line to Cimarron and Ute Park, causing the old town to come to life, particularly the section across the Cimarron River on the north side where real estate operators bought a townsite and erected hotels, stores, selling lots and houses to people who arrived with the rails.

Today there are still two Cimarrons, "old" and "new", divided by the river. All the historic buildings remaining are on the south side, including the jail and the famous 100-year-old granary built to hold the wheat produced on the Maxwell Grant. The notorious St. James Hotel, where owner Herbert Lambert, "had a man for breakfast twenty-six times", still stands in somewhat altered form as does the Don Diego Tavern. Across the street are the all but obliterated ruins of the Maxwell House.

Not far away is the Philmont Ranch, originally Kit Carson's Rayado Rancho established in 1849, later owned by Waite Philips. In 1941 the ranch was turned over to the National Boy Scouts. Now thousands of boys hold their annual Jamborees there, few realizing the aura of history surrounding old Cimarron.

THESE ARE AMONG FIRST of "new" Cimarron's buildings erected around 1905, now abandoned except for occasional use as rooming houses. Level rays of setting sun cast shadow of old cottonwood against side of weathered stone and brick structure.

DAWSON, NEW MEXICO

In a day when almost everybody burned wood in their stoves, J. B. Dawson was called a crackpot since he scraped chunks of coal from the surface of his farm land. Then out of curiosity, some of his neighbors asked for samples to burn and were pleased enough at the results to avoid the chore of bucking wood and buy the black fuel from Dawson.

J. B. Dawson, with his homestead, was one of the ranchers with a few hundred acres each who were giving trouble to the Maxwell Land Grant Company which had bought an immense tract from Lucien B. Maxwell. Having neglected to look into the matter of all the ranchers living on the land, they had no way of knowing who was a legal owner and who was merely squatting.

When the company saw the ground was heavily laced with coal, it hankered to develop the vein but the attempted eviction of Dawson brought him up fighting, claiming he had bought his land from Maxwell although admitting the transaction had been purely verbal, sealed with a handshake. Maxwell, he said, always did business that way, and the company officials found he was right.

Dawson was disposed to settle the matter with six-guns but consented to abide by a court decision. He hired attorney Andrieus A. Jones who was well aware of Maxwell's real estate deals. The case was tried in the fall of 1893 and decided in favor of

Dawson. The New Mexico Supreme Court held that the company could not prove that Dawson did not own the land, or mineral rights thereof, an important point since the coal deposits were the crux of the whole argument. Maxwell, of course, could not testify as he had died eighteen years earlier.

The trial brought out some facts that further added to the company's discomfort. Dawson stated he had paid Maxwell $3,700 for what he thought was 1,000 acres. The lawyer proved the date and amount were correct but the parcel of land embraced 20,000 acres.

Dawson set about marketing his coal in a big way, with his neighbors the Springers, selling the coal-bearing area to the newly organized Dawson Fuel Company for $400,000 and $5,000 for a township site. He held out 1200 acres on which to build a home, wishing to retain "a little open space around the house." By advice of counsel Dawson had all transactions in black and white with all signatures duly witnessed. But his wife would not sign until she obtained full rights to sell all milk, for a period of ten years, the anticipated town of Dawson would need. J. B. conceded.

Much of the development was under the control of C. B. Eddy, president of the El Paso and Northeastern Railroad, the man who had changed his mind about running his rails to the mining camp

SOLID STONE BARN for sheltering horses and equipment of Phelps Dodge Corp. was retained by company among others for huge cattle ranch when property was sold. This was in 1950 and sounded death knell for Dawson.

of White Oaks, feeling officials of that settlement were holding him up on land for right-of-way and depot. (See Ghost Town Album — Ed.) The railroad had gone to Carrizozo instead to tap coal beds there. These deposits proved shallow and now Eddy was anxious to recoup his losses in the expected deeper veins at Dawson.

On June 17, 1901, the Las Vegas OPTIC reported: "President C. B. Eddy of the El Paso and Northeastern, accompanied by a party of other railroad men, visited Colfax County last week to inspect the Dawson coal lands recently purchased by the El Paso and Northeastern road. Mr. Eddy, in an interview with a reporter with the Las Vegas OPTIC, stated that the money is on hand for the construction of a railroad to the coal fields, and the likelihood is that the railroad will miss Las Vegas a distance of fully twenty miles. A township has been purchased and laid out at the Dawson ranch by the new owners of the Dawson coal fields, as Mr. Eddy is a town builder and boomer who always gets there in his projects. It may be predicted that the new town in Colfax County, through his efforts backed by the railroad he represents, will become one of the most important towns in New Mexico." The company showed a capital of $1,900,000 divided into 10,000 shares with headquarters at Alamogordo where the railroad company already maintained offices.

The same year saw incorporation of the Dawson Railroad Company, also with headquarters at Alamogordo, with plans to build a railroad 130 miles long from Liberty to Dawson, taking advantage of some stretches of lines already constructed or building. Its heads were most of the people who had bought the Dawson coal lands.

Things began happening fast on that ground. By August 1, 1901 a crew of fifty miners was on hand to work the first vein outcropping. A sawmill was busy turning out lumber for houses and by the end of that first year Dawson was well on the way to becoming a city and center of the largest coal mining operation in New Mexico. A post office was established with George T. Pearl the first postmaster. There was a wine and liquor store owned by Henry Pfaff, a large store called the Southwestern Mercantile Co. The town doctor was H. K. Pangborn. By 1902 Dawson's population was 600, with 40 children in the new school. The place had a fine, stimulating climate, there was plenty of work for everyone and Dawson seemed blessed above many other towns. Yet it was doomed to suffer a series of tragedies that shadowed its history to the end.

The first of these struck on September 14, 1903. A fire and explosion in Mine No. 1 took a comparatively light toll, three trapped miners being killed, the bodies shipped away to the nearest known relatives. The worst blow did not come for ten years when Dawson had its cemetery.

1905 brought a newspaper, the Dawson NEWS, with enormous expansion of population and mine operations. There were now about 2,000 people living in the town and many new homes constructed. The Dawson Hotel got a 70-foot addition. Capacity of the coal washer was increased to 250 tons an hour, total number of coke ovens to 124. The mine company owned huge kilns, built mainly to produce bricks for coke ovens and chimneys. Coke, the solid portion remaining after coal is subjected to intense heat in a closed retort, was a major export to smelters and foundries all over the southwest. It burned with a pure flame without gas or smoke, being nearly pure carbon.

About this time the giant, omnipresent Phelps Dodge Corporation began to show a strong interest in what was going on at Dawson. It sent one of its best men, Dr. James Douglas, to the camp with the result the company bought the operation and organized the Stag Canyon Fuel Company, capitalized at $5 million. Under the new management the town expanded even more to a population of 3,500 and the "palatial" Dawson Theater was completed at a cost of $40,000.

Dawson's bawdy houses were forced to build additions to accommodate the large influx of single miners. Trouble ensued, as evidenced in an item in the Raton RANGE, August 15, 1907: "Lizzie Zeller, an inmate of one of the houses in the red light district of Dawson, was shot by Tom Jenkins over the accidental shooting of John Jenkins, his brother. John and Lizzie were in friendly dispute over a gun when the weapon went off and shot John. When Tom heard his brother was wounded he went to the house, called for the woman, called her vile names and shot her. He was placed under arrest. . . The Zeller woman will be taken to her home in Las Vegas for burial."

The camp was largely populated by foreign born workers — Greeks, Slavs, Italian, French, Welsh, Scotch, Mexicans, Germans, Japanese and Chinese. Most of the single men, and those who had to make a stake before sending for their wives, lived in a separate section called Boarding House Row. Greeks and Italians were numerous enough to have their own divisions, presided over by a boarding boss of their own nationality, since many had not yet learned to speak English.

The kilns supplying bricks for construction of coke ovens and chimneys also turned out material for rebuilding and modernizing the old frame school houses, one of the largest being Dawson High School with forty teachers. The Dawson Hospital, with a staff of five doctors, maintained a complete laboratory, with surgery and X-ray equipment. Buildings on the grounds housed nurses and other employees, kitchen, laundry and dispensary with registered pharmacist.

On April 6, 1913, the Raton REPORTER said: "The Phelps Dodge Company that owns the Stag Canyon Mines at Dawson has planned the reclamation of an immense area of land in the vicinity of Dawson by means of a reservoir and a system of ditches and canals, which when completed will be one of the largest irrigation projects in the country. The contract amounts to $350,000."

It was during this period of abundance and prosperity that Dawson suffered its worst catastrophe. On October 20, 1913, a tremendous explosion in Mine No. 2 clogged the entrances and entombed 300 men, killing 263. The blast came at 3 p.m. There were no warnings, no escaping gas or rumblings, only a sudden roar.

Relief and disaster crews were rushed from neighboring towns — Raton, Trinidad, Blossburg, Brilliant, Gardner, Van Houten and Morley. Even a relief car was sent from Denver. By 11 a.m. next day 22 men were accounted for, with 16 alive, and it was hoped this ratio of men saved would prevail, but as the days dragged on the recovered dead outnumbered the living. Rescue crews worked around the clock, rows of bodies brought to the surface grew longer, distraught wives and family members clogged and impeded operations around the mouth of the mine. Two of the rescuers were themselves killed by falling boulders in the shaft. Immense mass funerals were conducted for the victims and row upon row of graves dug, making it necessary to extend the cemetery far up the hill. Wholesale burials were not completed for weeks.

Even after such a calamity life and coal mining went on in the camp and in time, some of the festivities. The camp had always been a good show town and traveling theatrical companies found good audiences even shortly after the disaster.

The NEW MEXICO MAGAZINE, San Diego Exposition Souvenir Edition in 1915, carried a story on Dawson. It included such comments as: "Many a little flower garden surounds the cottage. Sometimes the earth where the cottage stands is hard and stony, and then it is a common thing for the resi-

dent of that house to wall his yard with stones, and then haul in rich earth for his garden. Men do not do these things when their tenure is uncertain. They keep their lawns cropped and the window boxes with their bits of bloom neatly painted. They do good work in the mines and are happy . . . the houses themselves are worthy of comment. There are no shacks. There is no poorer section, although there is a separate quarter for the non-English speaking. . . . .

"The Church, like the schools is financed by the company. There is only one, the Church of All Creeds, but services of several denominations are held in it. Rev. Harvey M. Shields, an Episcopal minister is in charge of regular services, but a Catholic priest holds services in the camp once a month. A Catholic church is being built." The Catholic church was completed in 1917 and dedicated to St. John the Baptist, with the Rev. Joseph A. Couturier, O.M.I. as first pastor.

Safety measures were heavily increased after the disastrous explosion and subsequent accidents were comparatively minor, fatalities few. But in February, 1923, another ruinous explosion took 125 lives. Again the cemetery had to be extended to allow more space for more rows of graves, the mass burial scenes of 1913 repeated.

No further tragedy took place until the one of February 25, 1950. On that date the people of Dawson were told the Phelps Dodge Corporation would close down all operations of the Stag Canyon Mining Co. The announcement meant the death of the one industry town. The reason for the closure was simple — the increasing availability of a new fuel for smelters and foundries, natural gas. Specifically the enormous Phelps Dodge copper smelter at El Paso, Texas, which had been consuming most of Dawson's coke output, now found it more expensive to produce than the handily obtainable natural gas.

When the final blow fell at the actual closure on April 30th, many residents had already left and vacant houses showed curtainless windows. The only surviving operation, and that a temporary one, was the Frontier Power Plant which served Dawson and surrounding area with electricity. It operated until a stock pile of surface coal was exhausted.

On June 6th, the National Iron and Metal Company of Phoenix, Arizona, bought the deserted town of Dawson, wrecking and removing all machinery and buildings. A few houses were spared, these and the land having been retained by Phelps Dodge for a large cattle operation.

DAWSON'S CEMETERY, several times expanded, is filled with grim reminders of many mine disasters. At least 400 miners were killed in series of cave-ins and explosions. Most graves are marked simply with company-provided metal crosses but some, as one on left, have distinctive family monuments. Polyglot languages spoken by miners from many lands are reflected in almost all markers as this one, marking resting place of worker from Modena, Italy.

KOEHLER, NEW MEXICO

The swastika, ancient symbol of good luck, seemed to cast its benediction on all of Koehler and its huge coal mines. The emblem was a part of life in the camp, seen on every building and all business correspondence, natural enough as the mining company was named Swastika Fuel Co. All this was pre-Hitler and while all signs and symbols were removed in war time, ghost town seekers may still be slightly puzzled at outlines and evidences of the swastika on some of Koehler's weathered boards.

In the spring of 1909 when the town's spectacular growth was attracting national attention, the Des Moines (Iowa) REGISTER sent reporter Tracy Garrett west to write a feature on it. The article was reprinted in the Santa Fe NEW MEXICAN, June 13, 1909, and later included in the works of historian F. Stanley, pseudonym of Francis L. Stanley Crocchiola. Native of New York, teacher of English, history and other subjects at St. John's College on the Hudson, Crocchiola came to New Mexico for his health, amassing a great store of the state's history and writing many books about it. He cites the REGISTER's story as containing the most vivid picture possible of life in Koehler, particularly on pay day.

"The miners are paid once a month, and though no credit is given, no one need go hungry or thirsty between paydays. This is avoided by a system of scrip money. After a miner has worked three days he can go to the mine office and draw a portion of his "time" in scrip. The scrip is elaborately lithographed paper in denominations of from ten cents to five dollars in scrip and good only for merchandise at the company store or saloon.

"From Raton comes the paymaster on the afternoon of payday. With him is a chest containing about $24,000 and three or four armed guards with six-shooters and Winchesters. The chest is carried into the company store and there closely guarded until 7:30, when the line that has been forming since early evening is permitted to enter.

"At the pay window, or directly in front of it sits Bill Bolden, marshall of the camp, deputy sheriff, gun man, a sure shot, a man who is always cool in danger, mild of voice, quick of action. At Bill's side hangs a six-shooter, but he seldom has to reach for it. Every man in camp knows that he can reach for it with lightning quickness, and no one dares to provoke him into action. A word from Bill Bolden will stop the line of march or a fight. He is all powerful at Koehler.

"For pay day and night and the day following several extra deputies are sworn in. Their badges of office are well filled cartridge belts, six-shooters and rifles. These men are much in evidence around the stores when the $24,000 is being handed out to the laborers. . . The cashier counts out the money, currency, except for the last four to seven dollars, this being paid in silver so the man may have some change handy when he leaves the window. . . .

"On the outskirts of the crowd, pushing and

STOCK PILE of coal at Koehler seems tremendous now in face of little demand, would be mere drop in bucket in days when all locomotives on lines of Atcheson, Topeka and Santa Fe were burning coal. Now little used spur line visible in middle ground runs to mine short distance above.

ONCE HUGE MINE OPERATION just above Koehler is still in limited production. Skeleton crew removes some coal, guards valuable machinery. Sometimes former miners bring children here for visit, try to explain working of tipples, cars, washers, usually meet with lack of interest.

jostling to keep as near the line as possible, are women of all nations waiting for the breadwinner money, that they may secure their share for the purchase of supplies or perhaps a ribbon or a piece of dress goods. Some, especially the Mexican and Italian women, are gaily dressed, green, red and yellow being the favorite colors, and she who can contrive to have all these colors on wears the happiest smile. One girl of fourteen, who was pointed out as a bride of one week, appeared on payday night in a green satin skirt reaching to but a few inches below her knees, red shoes and stockings, yellow waist, and a hat that combined all colors. As she was waiting for her newly wed husband to draw his wages a withered old lady forced her way through the crowd whispered to Bolden, and the payline was halted. The woman presented a time check for $7.50 and hurried over to the butcher

shop. Again the line moved on. Soon after another woman slipped up to the marshall and the performance was repeated. Every few minutes this occurred, with never a word of complaint from the waiting miners. For these women were the wives of miners who were ill or had been injured. . . .

"The throng of recently paid representatives of a dozen nations left the women and picked their way up the track to where the saloon door stood invitingly open. The saloon is tremendous barn-like structure running more than one hundred feet down a side. Crowded three and four deep about the bar were negroes, Chinamen, Slavs, Greeks and Mexicans, in fact all nations except Japs. The other side of the room is lined with card tables and these two are crowded with players of everything from stud poker to cooncan. Before them sat their mugs and glasses and among them hurried sturdy waiters,

selected for their jobs as much for their ability to bounce disturbers as for filling empty glasses. A babel of languages rose from the tables and bar, and could be heard across the prairie and towards the ranches long after the lights of the town were left behind and only the glare from the coke ovens marked for the eye the place where payday night was at its height.

"Sunday the day following pay night was quiet at the town. Riding through the gate that surrounds the camp, there were, however, many silent evidences of the revels of the night before. Empty and broken bottles, articles of clothing and pieces of harness. In the middle of the road, his coat folded carefully over his arm, his hat missing, lay a man, or the wreck of one. The sun shone brightly on his face, but though the hours passed, he did not move. Riders and drivers turned their horses aside, but none touched him. He was not dead, the marshall or one of his deputies would pick him up. 'Every-

thing passed off nice', remarked the chief officer of the camp, as he kicked his boots on the store steps. "There wasn't a killing, or even a big fight, we have an all-fired peaceful outfit here in the lay-out.'" The writer expressed himself as confident however that any lack of fights and killings could be credited to Bill Bolden and his pair of six-shooters rather than to any inherent restraint on the part of the miners.

Koehler had no more fire protection than any of the mining camps and time after time large sections of the town were destroyed, one of the last disasters, in 1923, leveling the large two-story school building that served for twenty years. By the start of the new year the community hall or other structures were sufficiently remodeled to serve as pro-tem school houses.

Yet the town might have saved itself the trouble. The mines closed down in 1924 and that meant desertion of the camp. Koehler became a ghost town

RUINS OF CATHOLIC CHURCH in Morley, Colorado, just north of state line. Miss Zoe Henion, now of Portland, Oregon, clerked in Trinidad general store, remembers Morley miners had to buy own blasting powder, caps etc. Worst mine disaster was in 1910 when 97 men were killed. "Funerals were held in batches of ten at a time," Miss Henion recalls. "The victims were buried in Trinidad as Morley had no cemetery." Workers in Morley were mostly Mexicans, some uneducated Indians. Company provided many comforts in homes, such as plumbing and bathtubs. Annual inspection for cleanliness, proper care of improvements revealed one bathtub filled with potatoes.

KOEHLER had cosmopolitan population of about 1,200. Houses were heated with free coal, lit by kerosene in early days. When electricity became available company insisted on electric lights, forbade old lamps clung to by many foreign born workers and families. Times also changed shopping habits, residents forsaking local stores to travel to large centers at Raton and Trinidad, Colorado, when rapid transportation became available.

and remained empty for twelve years. Then with some returning demand for coal the owners decided to reactivate conservatively. Mr. J. Van Houten, head of the company made a public statement to stockholders. "As this property has been idle since 1924 many repairs to tracks, buildings and pipelines will be necessary. Considerable new equipment will have to be purchased. For this purpose the sum of $200,000 has been appropriated by the board. By adding production of this mine to that of existing operations, the company's producing capacity will be maintained for many years to come." Mr. Koehler's report went on to stress new expenses added to the company's outlay, such as increased taxes, unemployment contributions, social security costs. "The recent increase in oil prices will help some," he said with a qualifying note, "to what extent remains to be seen."

That was in 1938 and actual reopening of the mine was still postponed. The Atcheson, Topeka and Santa Fe, previously the largest single purchaser of coal for its locomotives, was rapidly converting to oil. More, government control of coal processing was not favorable to mine owners.

Finally, for a few years, the company produced coal again but on a very limited scale. Production in 1954 was only 57,000 tons, almost all used for fuel in neighboring towns. "The railroads are now almost completely dieselized as far as locomotive power is concerned," wailed the president. "We have been unsuccessful in securing any government contracts of consequence. We have tried to interest the authorities in shipments of coal to Japan and other foreign destinations but to no avail."

The neighboring coal camp of Van Houten, one of the largest in the northern New Mexico complex, closed down February 2, 1954. At first related camps felt the closure would improve their own situations but creeping paralysis set in. Brilliant, where investment was over $1 million at one time, was soon affected as was its close neighbor Gardner. It was only a matter of time until Koehler, already ailing, would receive the kiss of death. The same fate was in store for Catskill, Yankee, Blossburg, Carisburg and Morley, just across the line in Colorado.

The common denominator in the death of New Mexico's coal camps was the failing usefulness of solid fuels, variations being only in detail. Where coke was the major product as in Dawson, its use in foundries was replaced by natural gas. Where raw coal was the big export, as in Koehler and other camps, it was diesel oil that rang the death knell.

GARDINER and adjacent neighbor, Brilliant, part of northern New Mexico coal mining complex, died when mines were closed July 29, 1953. Company destroyed many buildings to reduce or eliminate value and taxes. Here as in other coal towns, much early construction was of readily available adobe, traditional building material among New Mexico's large Spanish and Mexican population.

COLFAX PREDATED most of coal towns in Colfax County, was only a stop on the old road to Cimarron, a flourishing supply center while Dawson, a short distance up the canyon, boomed with its coal production. When railroad was built directly to coal mines at Dawson, Colfax declined. Town is now deserted except for family living in old Frederici store, built and operated by father of Fred Frederici, District Judge of Raton, now deceased. Senior Frederici migrated to America from Italy in 1903, remembered when coke ovens glowed at nearby Starkville, Colorado, now "suburb" of Trinidad.

COLFAX GRADE SCHOOL. Judge Frederici came to Colfax at high school age, traveled up canyon to Dawson for classes. Younger brother, sister, two Frederici cousins attended this grade school as did two Dickman boys and numerous progeny of railroad section hands. Judge Frederici recalled: "There never was a church at Colfax, although I attended the occasional services in the school building."

DICKMAN HOTEL, reminder of Colfax prosperity when A.T. & S.F. and S.P. railroads crossed there, bringing much transient business.

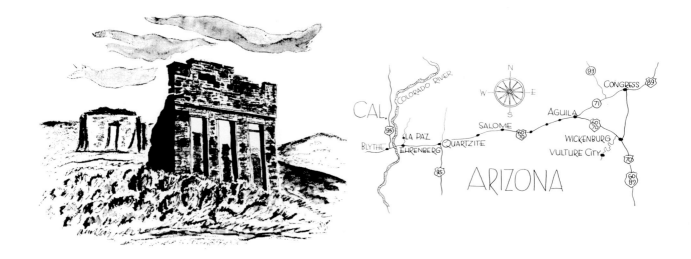

EHRENBERG, ARIZONA

Whiskey, loose women, pigs and the law were all mixed up in Tom Hamilton's life. He served some of the whiskey over the bar and drank about the same amount to keep it from spoiling. Loose women were no problem as long as he could get enough customers for them. But his pigs caused the judge no end of trouble — and he was the judge.

Hamilton ran a combination store, saloon and brothel in Ehrenberg, a brawling frontier town in the late '60s and through the '70s. The drab cluster of adobe buildings was not a mining town but served as a supply center for the placer activity along the Colorado River's east shore.

As a bartender, Hamilton set up the bottles and glasses, pawed in the money and gold dust and took three fingers himself when anybody wanted to pay for it. And if there were fights and shootings, he was no man to stop the boys from having a little fun. Somebody was bound to be thrown in the calaboose and who would he face in the court in the morning? Tom Hamilton, justice of the peace.

That is, if and providing the j.p. was sober enough to face anybody. If not, he was regaining his strength in bed and further derelict in another duty — looking after his pigs. The porkers had no respect for the flimsy fence around the sty and were not inclined to lead their lives in quiet desperation. They wandered. And most of the time into stores to root around in the leather, lamp wicks and lard and cause general consternation. They also invaded private kitchens and found no welcome greetings from the women trying to get a pot of beans in the oven.

Complaints became so numerous the judge decided he would have to do something but nothing as drastic as staying sober to look after his swine. He simply commandeered a raft, took the pigs across the Colorado and turned them loose. They had to be content rooting around in the willows, until the happy day they discovered a prospector's camp and reduced the food supply to a shambles. The prospector evened things up by shooting one of the vandals and hanging the butchered carcass to a convenient tree branch.

But these goings on were witnessed by one of the Indians in the j.p.'s employ and he reported them to Hamilton. Already unsteady, the owner of the pigs downed a couple more, groped for his gun, crossed the river and found the guilty pig shooter still in camp and very indignant. "This is California," he protested to Hamilton with a show of bravado. "Your jurisdiction is good only in Arizona and you can't force me to cross the river." The judge responded that his gun said he could and he did.

The hearing was held in the saloon immediately. Tom Hamilton lubricated his throat and made a speech to the effect that the prospector was now in Arizona where he was subject to the law laid down by Ehrenberg's justice of the peace. He had stolen and killed a pig belonging to the said jurist and the crime had been witnessed. Nobody could say he had

ALMOST COMPLETE ANONYMITY is lot of pioneers buried in old Ehrenberg cemetery. The good markers of wood have long since weathered away, as many carried off by souvenir hunters, those remaining showing little or no legend, as board at left. Sometimes cacti, such as cholla, right center, afford a sort of temporary monument. One grave is said to have been marked: "J.C. 1867", with brand of the man's horse and year he died of gunplay in street.

not had a fair trial so the penalty was fair — to Hamilton. "I fine you $50 for stealing and $50 for the hog."

In New Mexico Territory in January, 1862, Captain Pauline (born Paulino) Weaver discovered some flakes of gold in a wash called by the Mexicans Arroyo Del Tinaja. The location was roughly halfway between what would later be Ehrenberg and Quartzsite, some 140 miles north of Yuma (then Arizona City) on the Colorado. Weaver is said to have secreted the gold in a goose quill pen for safekeeping but the legend does not explain how he happened to have such an object in his possession as he was illiterate. The yellow granules were taken to Yuma where their glint created a sensation and started a full-scale gold rush.

Jose Maria Redondo was in the vanguard. He found a nugget, called by the Mexicans *chispa,* weighing two ounces. When he spread the news in Yuma a second exodus depopulated the town even more. Then in February Juan Ferra discovered a *chispa* of nearly three pounds.

Now the news spread to the coast and the cities of Los Angeles and San Francisco began to feel the impact with so many hopefuls leaving for the gold fields on the Colorado. But now came an obstacle almost unique in gold rush history — the blazing heat. The climate had been most pleasant in January but by July the hordes of would-be miners ar-

riving from the cool coast found temperatures rising to 120 degrees, with suffocating humidity from the river and its vegetation. There were many heat prostrations and some deaths, particularly among women and children.

Many were discouraged, many returned to the coast, replaced by hardy Mexicans from Sonora. Then a nugget was displayed in the window of a California jeweler, C. Ducommun. The glittering curiosity weighed almost four pounds. This reversed the traffic flow and soon there were so many travelers arriving at the riverbank that enterprising William Bradshaw established a ferry and reaped a harvest comparable to those in the placers where hardly a man made less than $100 a day, some $1,000.

Soon a town came into being as a center for supplies and liquid refreshment — Laguna de la Paz, shortened to La Paz. Olivia, Mineral City and Ehrenberg sprang up nearby, only the latter reaching any size. Laguna de la Paz or "Lake of Peace" was bordered by a quiet backwater of the Colorado when founded, yet the valley became a menace, anything but peaceful, when the floods came roaring down. Olivia was named for "Ollie" Oatman, one of two sisters who were taken into brutal captivity by Apaches near Gila Bend in 1851 when their parents were killed and brother badly beaten. The other sister, Mary Ann, died while held by the

FRAGMENT OF ADOBE BUILDING at left is sole remaining reminder of many such structures once lining several streets of flourishing river port of Ehrenberg.

Indians but Olivia was released in 1856 and joined her brother who by then had recovered in Yuma. Mineral City was hopefully named when good deposits of gold ore were panned in the nearby wash, booming for a short time and dying as the metal petered out.

Ehrenberg lived longer. Herman Ehrenberg, mining engineer and hero of the Texas Independence War, was a famous figure in early Arizona history, having prospected almost all the state. Right after the Gadsden Purchase he and another well known Arizona pioneer, Charles D. Poston, spent some of 1854 and 1855 looking over the hills above Tubac. Ehrenberg gradually worked his way northwest toward the placers along the gullies and washes.

"Mike" Goldwater, grandfather of the present senator, had a business in La Paz. It flourished with the town but when mud deposits cut it from the river about 1869 the place began to falter and Goldwater established a new store six or seven miles down the Colorado where a number of adobe houses had been erected around an army post installed ten years earlier. He named the new town for his longtime friend Ehrenberg who had been murdered at Dos Palmas.

Until 1877 when the railroad reached and passed beyond Yuma, the store of J. Goldwater & Bro. was supplied mainly by river boats plying the Colorado, returning downstream with many pounds of placer gold for the San Francisco mint. The light boats went down to Puerto Ysabel at the mouth of the river, their cargo shifted to ocean-going vessels for the voyage down the Gulf of California and north to San Francisco. Several of the river boats were owned by Capt. Isaac Polhamus under the name of the Colorado Steam Navigation Co. He and the Goldwater brothers were cronies, for although Polhamus lived in Yuma, he was often in Ehrenberg with one of his steamers.

The town was so well supplied with saloons it could spare one. When forced out of business for lack of patronage, the building was put into use as a school house, the town's first. In April, 1872, bright-eyed Mary Elizabeth Post came from San Diego by stagecoach to Yuma where she waited ten days for the flat-bottomed boat to take her to Ehrenberg as its first teacher. Barely settled in the raw, dusty frontier town, Mary Elizabeth was confronted by fifteen bashful, dark-eyed Mexican children, none of whom could speak a word of English — and she no word of Spanish. She was rescued by the kindly owner of the store next door who took over as interpreter. In addition to formal lessons,

OLD PHOTO OF LA PAZ taken at turn of century shows long abandoned river port as ghost town. Buildings were adobe, only material available. Town was originally called Laguna de la Paz, situated on backwater lagoon of Colorado River. Harbor proved liability, filling with sand when river became raging torrent in unusually high water from melting snows in Rockies. Isolation from vital river traffic proved fatal to port.

pupils and teacher sat outside in the evenings with lights out so as not to attract insects and did exercises in language and poetry.

Living was rugged in Ehrenberg. All water had to be hauled from the muddy Colorado and settled in tanks. Four inches of dust lay in the street and building lumber was imported at great cost, the only local trees being scrubby willows and cottonwoods. Construction was almost entirely adobe and sundried bricks whose thickness gave some protection from the hot sun. Insects were obnoxious, especially the stinging, biting types and non-biting black flies that swarmed in black clouds over all food. Part of the plague was due to garbage decomposing at the edge of town in the intense heat and there were always burro and cattle droppings.

Yet as long as gold was harvested nearby and as long as river traffic was important, Ehrenberg continued to thrive. But the $7 million in gold panned out of the arroyos was all there was. When the railroad was completed past Yuma the river boats lost their lifeline and stayed tied to the wharves. Olivia and Mineral City succumbed, leaving almost no trace.

MONUMENT IN EHRENBERG CEMETERY, built of stone, topped by Indian petroglyphic rock, fifteen feet in height, space around base left for pioneer relics. The dedication address was made June 10, 1934 by W. S. Simms of Phoenix, 1500 people gathering from all parts of California and Arizona to hear it. A copper tablet was placed at base reading: "This monument erected to preserve the memory of pioneers and adventurers resting in these unmarked graves." Plate has long since been pried off by vandals, attempts made to remove gold pans and other relics from base. Construction was done by state highway employees.

Ehrenberg has almost vanished too. Until a very few years ago there were numerous adobe ruins standing forlornly near the river to give some semblance of shape to the once busy port. Then came a trailer park and the historic remains were leveled to the ground, except for one pitiful corner remnant still visible from the road. The cemetery is somewhat more permanent although most markers have vanished and the legends on the few remaining ones are illegible.

La Paz is even more nebulous. It gave up the county seat to Yuma in 1870 and quickly faded out. A few mounds of adobe remain at the edge of the Colorado River Indian Reservation six miles above Ehrenberg, almost impossible to find in the brush and sand.

WAGON HAS STOOD near cemetery many years, protracted weathering making pattern of wood grain.

CHARLES TYSON was one of earliest settlers at Tyson's Wells, original site of town of Quartzsite. Generous springs of good water had previously been used by Mojave Indians who resented intrusion of whites. To protect themselves, settlers petitioned U.S. Army to build fort. Government constructed this adobe building to house small contingent of soldiers, never a regular army post, it nevertheless served the purpose.

QUARTZSITE, ARIZONA

Hi Jolly and eighty camels crossing the desert sands of Arizona furnish the color behind the settlement of Quartzsite at Tyson's Well. The camel caravans did not stay in the country but Hi Jolly did, to act as scout for the army and he lies buried in an unmarked grave in the local cemetery.

The town came into being because gold was found between that spot, Ehrenberg and La Paz. While never a mining camp it was an important stage stop, at first with no name but because of a well there and a man named Tyson the first settler, it became known as Tyson's Well. When the Indians began a series of attacks on the few residents, an adobe fort was installed with a few soldiers and the place became Fort Tyson although it was never a formal army fort.

In time the settlement needed a post office but authorities rejected the name Fort Tyson as having no standing. The white nature of the prevailing country rock suggested "Quartzite" which name was accepted, but somewhere along the line an "s" was inserted and the infant town became officially Quartzsite. This was the area adopted by Hi Jolly who had been Hadji Ali in Syria.

About 1855 the United States Government decided to use camels to open up the road from Fort Defiance to the Colorado River, the country almost all desert. Civilian Gynn Harris Heap was sent to the Middle East to procure camel herds and bring them home. He centered his search in Smyrna, Turkey, and frequented a grog shop called Mimico Teadora near the famous Caravan Bridge where Arabs and Greeks gathered in friendly talk.

Here in late 1856 Heap met his man, one Hadji Ali who had spent most of his life with camels, half of it driving or buying them for others. The first packet of camels had been readied for the voyage and Hadji Ali was ready to leave with them on his great adventure. Instead he was sent into the interior of Asia Minor to secure a second herd and then accompanied it to the United States, arriving at Indianola, Texas, February 10, 1857.

Hi Jolly as he now was called never spoke much of his past but friends and army men knew his father was an Arabian who had participated in a raid on a Greek island and taken a native girl as a trophy of war. She became Hadji Ali's mother and for a time he went by the Greek name Philip Tetro, later changing it when he embraced the Mohammedan faith.

The two shipments of camels comprised groups of thirty-three and forty-seven, several females bringing forth young aboard ship. The herd was divided into several units and under Arab drivers taken over snowy mountains, through pine woods and over deserts, covering about twenty-five miles a day. The camels did not protest at the heavy packs but the drivers did. One by one they quit but Hi Jolly stayed on to break in new drivers from army personnel.

The camel project seemed to be going well but the Civil War broke out to end it, road building and all. The camels were offered as "surplus" but there were almost no takers. The animals required special handling, were crankier than mules and panicked other stock. Turned loose to fend for themselves they got along with varying degrees of success. Myths and legends about the strange beasts grew rapidly, one concerning "a great, rusty-red animal" seen mysteriously with a dead rider strapped to its back. As the beast roamed the wastelands pieces of the body were torn off against brush and cacti until only the legs and then only the feet remained. At last someone shot the wanderer which by then carried only the rawhide bindings. Another engaging legend was offered by Indians. One camel was foolish enough to defy the spirits of thunder and lightning, was turned into stone and the origin of Camelback Mountain near Phoenix explained.

With the abandonment of the camels, Hi Jolly was out of a job, but not for long as he was too good a man as scout and guide in Northern Arizona with which he was now familiar. He keeps appearing in stories about the subjugation of the Indians by the army and the rounding up of cattle and horse thieves.

About 1871 a band of Apaches stole over a hundred head of horses, mules and cattle from the

Bowers Ranch in Skull Valley, killing the herder in the process. Hi Jolly was working at Fort Mc-Dowell and was sent out as tracker for a cavalry company. He came across the trail but could not persuade the commanding officer it was the right one. Disgustedly he returned to the Fort and when the soldiers returned the officer was arrested and courtmartialed.

On April 28, 1880, Hi Jolly was married to Gertrude Serna of Tucson, in that city. The marriage started out well but the Greek-Arab was a born nomad, the trait kept alive by years of scouting and prospecting. In 1894 he reported in Yuma that he had located a rich deposit of tin in the Plomosa district. He had been living in the Tyson's Wells area, he said, and made the discovery in seeking medical aid for a sick prospector who had been working with him. His final wanderings were confined to the Tyson's Well or Quartzsite area where he died, December 16, 1902.

MONUMENT TO HI JOLLY, dedicated January 5, 1936. Built by Arizona Highway Department, copper camel at apex was made in Highway shops at Phoenix. Memorial stands in Quartzsite Cemetery where, in unmarked grave, lies famed camel driver, scout and prospector. Base rocks are black lava of the area, next above snowy quartzite, then band of petrified wood. Rounded log section near right corner is spectacular specimen, ruby red in color, proves vandals sometimes have self-control. In copper container at base are Hi Jolly's government contracts, ashes of Topsy, one of his camels which died at Griffith Park Zoo in Los Angeles, and his total wealth at death — sixty cents.

SALOME, ARIZONA

The Salome Frog, second in fame only to Mark Twain's Celebrated Frog of Calaveras County, was the creation of Dick Wick Hall. He made the frog known locally through the pages of his little weekly newspaper, the SALOME SUN, then in the late '20s broke him into the big time in the SATURDAY EVENING POST. The character was his talisman, symbol of his free spirit and sense of humor as big as the desert itself.

"The Salome Frog is seven years Old," he explained in one of his sketches which was accompanied by a cartoon showing the frog with a canteen on its back, "and even though he can't swim it isn't his Fault. He never had a chance, but he lives in Hope. Three years ago Fourth of July Palo Verde Pete shot off a box of Dynamite and the Frog thinking it was Thunder, chased the Cloud of Smoke two miles down the road, hoping it might rain. He is older and wiser now, and is getting like the rest of the Natives, he just sits and Thinks."

The frog of Salome wasn't born in that town, Hall went on to explain. He found its egg in Owens Valley in California and thought at first it was a wild duck egg, but on the way home it hatched and proved to be a frog. The creature was nurtured on loving care and bottled Shasta and Pluto water which explains why it grew up to be so healthy and active.

If not the founder of Salome, Dick Wick Hall was at least its moving force with his newspaper and service station where he sold "Laffing Gas." As De Forest Hall he was born in Creston, Iowa, 1877. After college he served in a war and collected rattlesnakes in Florida. At a Nebraska State Fair he was so entranced by a display of the Hopi Indians of Arizona, he set his sights on the northern part of the state, arriving there at twenty-one with $14.35 in his pocket. Very soon he was among the Hopis as a census taker and the Indians liked him so well he was taken into the tribe. Wearing Hopi garb, he studied their habits, customs and ceremonies including the sacred Snake Dance. Close observation of their drawings, petroglyphs and symbolic designs may have influenced his later use of sketches in his mimeographed paper the SALOME SUN.

After the Hopi interlude, Hall settled down for a time on a small ranch in Pleasant Valley, the area long the scene of a range feud between cattle and sheep ranchers, theoretically finished with a full-scale battle in 1887. Smaller outbursts continued periodically but Hall, growing vegetables for the community, was never involved. "I was never shot at," he said. "I guess good gardeners were too scarce."

Then came a stint on a construction job, followed by something more fitting to his talents. He was made editor of the WICKENBURG NEWS-HERALD, a paper of shaky stature which did not strengthen

BLUE ROCK INN, operated in days of Dick Wick Hall by Mrs. E. S. Jones and her three daughters. As girls married, husbands provided extra help when business boomed as highway was built by town. Hall wrote free "ad" in his paper: "All inside rooms have Running Water ready to run on Very Short Notice and by coming at the right Season of the Year you can have whichever You Prefer—Hot or Cold (always hottest in summer). Only the Ground and Atmosphere are provided with outdoor Rooms, as no covering is Needed in the summer Season which is often quite Long."

DICK WICK HALL'S MODEST HOME also served as shop where he mimeographed famous little paper, the **Salome Sun**. In 1926 Hall went to Los Angeles "unwillingly" to have dental work done and while there doctors discovered a far advanced case of Bright's Disease from which he died. His body lies under monument in front yard, shaft built of pieces of valuable ore which mining friends contributed. Two small boys guided photographer to spot, took exception to his pronunciation of town's name—Salomay—informed him correct way to say it was—Salom.

financially during his tenure. No doubt he contributed color with such doggerel as:

"The past ten months serve to remind us
Editors don't stand a chance.
The more work the more we find behind us
Bigger patches in our pants."

During his stay in Wickenburg he used the alliterative "Dick Wick" as his name and was Dick Wick Hall the rest of his days. Also during this period he was bitten by the prospecting bug and the condition became chronic. He wrote home so glowingly of his new love, Arizona, his brother Ernest (later to be Arizona's Secretary of State) joined him and the two started combing the surrounding hills with pick and pan. An acquaintance, one Shorty Alger, lit his fuse in a gopher hole in the area just west of Wickenburg and exposed a pocket of gold assaying $100 to the pound. The news set off a minor gold rush but Dick, being astute and on the spot, filed on 100,000 acres of desert land with his brother as partner.

Shorty's fifteen-foot hole soon yielded $30,000 worth of gold, then pinched out. With almost everyone going home, Dick stayed on and began the drilling of a well, determined to develop a town in

the area. Natural promotion qualities asserted themselves and when the well produced, he formed the Grace Valley Irrigation district.

Having struck some color close by he started a mine called the Glory Hole and as a few buildings sprang up, a town of sorts was born. The railroad was being run through from Wickenburg and he induced a merchant friend, E. S. Jones, former owner of stores in Wickenburg and old Congress, to set up a new one on his property to serve the railroad men and anyone happening along. The location was half a mile below the well and mine, more convenient to the railroad, so the buildings of the first settlement were moved down and new ones added. The tiny hamlet was named Salome for Grace Salome Pratt, wife of one of Dick's mining partners, Carl Pratt.

One addition to the slowly growing Salome was a boarding house and hotel run by Mrs. Jones and her three daughters—Evvy, Lucy and Dorothy. Another was a post office with Hall as temporary postmaster, and a saloon. Salome did not support the latter and it was reopened as a school. The first teacher was one of the Jones girls whose married sister in Wickenburg had several children of school age. When the roster got low the teacher would call her sister to send down the number needed to fill the necessary quota of eight.

Part of this time Dick Wick Hall was busy traveling through Louisiana, Texas, Utah, California and Florida promoting other interests which included mines, oil wells and real estate. When the highway was built close to Salome, paralleling the railroad, he saw possibilities in a gasoline station and garage, and began staying home to develop them. The road was rough and many tired travelers elected to spend the night at the Blue Rock Inn — the boarding house and hotel. Salome had been built north of the tracks and as the highway was run south of them, the store was left "stranded" as it were. Mr. Jones' enterprising sons-in-law, of which there were several by now, tried to prevail on the old gentleman to move the store to the highway. The patriarch was adamant. "Nothing doing. Let them come over here. They know where we are."

It was to publicize the gas station that Hall started his famous one-sheet mimeographed "newspaper" where the Salome Frog found a home. It was only one of many quizzical characters to appear on the pages. As prominent was Salome herself. She was early separated from the lady of the same name, being a ribald caricature of the Biblical dancer. Hall's masthead was varied, most often reading: "The Salome Sun, where she danced," followed by the disclaimer: "It wasn't my fault. I *told* her the Sand would be too hot without her shoes." Many free "ads" were shaped up to the benefit and sometimes embarrassment of the parties involved. One issue said you could always have hot or cold running water at the Inn, provided you came at the right season. Of the fertile soil around Salome, Hall wrote: "The Melons don't do too well here. The vines grow so fast they wear out the melons dragging them over the ground." He also said: "Salome's population has increased 100% a year — 19 people in 19 years", and one of his many comments about the aridity of the region was: "We plant onions between the potatoes, they make the eyes of the potatoes water enough to irrigate the garden." He made crude little maps for his customers at the Laffing Gas Station with a small line under them — "This map doesn't show all the bumps and curves, but don't worry, you will find them all right."

Salome today is still about the same size but many of the buildings are unoccupied. The vitality of the town faded with Hall's death in 1926. But both the town and Dick Wick Hall's spirit come to life each fall, September 10, with an old-fashioned pit barbecue, square and folk dances for the farmers and cattlemen for fifty miles around. They come with their families and relive the times of Dick Wick Hall. The paved roads are about the only difference from the days when he was writing:

"This very old Typewriter I learned to Type on has lost lots of its teeth. It was so Old and so many of its Letters were Gone that I got used to hitting the Capitals where the little ones were gone that I can't get Out of the Habit."

STORE ON HALL PROPERTY was set up by his friend E. S. Jones, former merchant of Wickenburg and old Congress, in 1906. Post office was added shortly, Hall serving as temporary postmaster. Little false-fronts stand silent and empty, slowly falling victims to weather.

VULTURE CITY, ARIZONA

In the center of a sun-baked plaza in Vulture City stands an imposing group of ancient stone buildings and in the floor of the central one is a cavernous stone-lined pit covered by a heavy iron door. At the height of activity at the Vulture mine in the 1880s the buildings also housed the general and assay offices and the stone chamber was used to store gold bullion for safekeeping until it could be shipped to Phoenix.

There was the day three horsemen with two pack horses rode up to the front of the bullion room. Two were the brothers Valenzuela, Inocente and Francisco. When they leveled guns and roughly demanded the iron door be raised, a guard and the superintendent protested. They were both shot and killed on the instant. While one of the bandits held a gun on the rest of the office force, the other two went into the bullion room, lifted the conveniently unlocked door, removed $75,000 worth of gold bars and loaded the boxes on the pack horses. Gunfire now broke out on both sides. A bullet hit one of the bandits who dropped to the dust while the other two fled with the gold.

A posse was hastily organized but by the time the pursuers caught up with their quarry the loot had been buried. The leader of the posse shot one of the desperadoes but was held back from killing the other who fled into the mesquite. For two months the fugitive was hounded but eventually he thought it was safe to return to the spot where the bullion was hidden. As he started to lift out the heavy bars, he was shot and fell across them.

For a few years after this the bullion was shipped out by Wells Fargo carriers. The stages were repeatedly held up, drivers killed and the gold carried off. This happened so often Wells Fargo officials declined to haul the cargo and the mining company resorted to packing it on horses over rough and devious routes across the desert. After these safe carries, the gold was sent over the road again and on the very first trip the stage was held up, both driver and guard killed.

This was the way things went at the Vulture from beginning to end. Violence of every sort haunted the mine, its many operators and the men who worked in the tunnels. Danger from raiding Apaches was everpresent, guards with ready rifles being stationed on the knolls surrounding the workings. Even so more than four hundred whites were killed by Indians in one fifteen-year period. Near the point where the road turned toward town, the Wickenburg-Ehrenberg stage was once ambushed, six passengers killed, two escaping. One of these was a woman who later died of her wounds. Robbery, murder and rape were so frequent in the camp itself that at least nineteen men were hanged from the gnarled ironwood tree in the plaza.

It all started with Heinrich Heintzel who had known there was a nice vein of coal on his father's land in Austria and had always wanted to mine and sell it, the family finances seeming ever at the vanishing point. His father stubbornly refused and after his death young Heinrich found out why. He dug some coal and sold it only to learn government agents would imprison him for not turning it over to them. He fled to America, changed

PART OF VULTURE CITY. On descending hill where are located deep shafted mine, shops and mills, much of town comes into view. Group of stone buildings at left faces other direction on central plaza. At extreme left is store, next taller structure contained general offices, smaller one next is bullion room with vault in floor, last is elaborate assay office with almost all equipment still intact. During one period of ore shortage several buildings were torn down, walls put through mill and much gold recovered. Present mine owner estimates "there are 25 to 35 thousand dollars worth of gold in the walls of these buildings remaining." Just beyond is frame building housing mess hall. Others are bunk and tool houses. At extreme right small stone building with vanishing shingles may have served as jail. At its left corner is hanging tree.

FENCE OF OCOTILLO CANES made by inserting them in rocky soil, binding them together with wire. Survival-sure plants have taken root and grown to normal height. Leafless in normally dry periods, wands have leafed out during rains in previous month, are now in brilliant November sun.

his name to Henry Wickenburg, headed for the West and started prospecting in Arizona.

He arrived in Yuma in 1862, having made arrangements to join the party of Major Van Bibber at La Paz to prospect in Peeples Valley. Low water in the Colorado delayed the boat so long young Henry found the major had departed without him. He started out after the party.

Here was a man fresh from a foreign land attempting to penetrate two hundred miles of strange desert land alone. It was an incredible effort but young Wickenburg accomplished it, finding Van Bibber and the others camped in Peeples Valley. They prospected along the Hassayampa River with little or no success and in 1864 several members gave up, the party reduced to six. While they stayed in the river camp to decide what to do next, the young and persistent Austrian headed his burro toward a peak, near which he had heard was a vein of gold.

He stopped a short distance from the peak and set up a semi-permanent camp with a small tent. After several days of prospecting he wanted to sweep out the floor, and since there were many vultures circling around, he shot one to get a wing for a good broom. The wounded bird was thrashing in the dust and as he killed it he saw under the fluttering wings bright glints of gold, Wildly excited, he gathered up several pieces of the rich ore, returned to his companions and filed a claim with them. All

went to work on the site but the drudgery and lack of water discouraged the five partners and after ten weeks they decamped.

Wickenburg named his mine and the lonely peak Vulture and set to work by himself. All winter he used pick and shovel to remove surface ore, stuffing it into rawhides and packing it on the backs of two burros to the Hassayampa, twenty miles away.

Mining the ore was not too difficult for at first he did not have to go below ground. The lode was almost pure quartz, actually projected from the ground to a height of eighty feet, the ridges providing roosting places for the vultures, and extended horizontally three hundred feet, sixty to eighty in width. This exposure of such rich, gold-bearing ore was unique and would affect the history of Arizona for years.

Being unable to hand crush his ore and pan it in the river with any efficiency, Wickenburg employed Charles Genung to help him build an arrastra, the crudest type of grinder. After Henry had sluiced some of the product in the river water, he was convinced he really had wealth if he could only mine and recover at the same time. So he engaged several willing men to do the digging, hauling the ore down to him at the stream where he built several more crushers. This was Wickenburg's first mistake and set the pattern for a whole series of heartbreaks.

SUPPER REMNANTS LEFT FOR 21 YEARS. When gold mining was curtailed by government some "bootlegging" was being done here under guise of milling ore hauled in from old copper mine nearby. Informed of illegal gold operations here, U. S. inspectors stopped the men but allowed them to get supper. After hurried meal culprits slipped away to neighboring Bagdad copper mine where they were employed, went to work on morning shift.

Since he had never had an assay run, Henry did not know just how rich his mine was. As the prospectors and miners dug into the lode they soon ran into ore worth $100,000 to the ton or better than 25% gold. It was too much to keep men honest and they diverted the richest ore, sending the rest down to the boss.

In spite of this there was enough good ore arriving at the Hassayampa to warrant the building of real stamp mills by various firms. One was erected and operated by the Goldwater brothers who owned the large store in La Paz and later in Ehrenberg. Before long there were four hundred and fifty wagons hauling ore and eighty-five mills to grind it, a far cry from Henry's sledge hammer days a short time before.

Lack of water at the mine was a continuing problem. It had to be hauled from the river and cost ten cents a gallon for both men and mules. The animals hauling the water got very thirsty in the dust and heat and drank most of it. And they also ate much hay which could not be grown in this sterile rocky area. Eventually the water problem was solved by pumping it from the Hassayampa and feed was produced in the fertile Salt River Valley, a small village growing up there. The first building was Hancock's Store and the name of the town became Phoenix.

Wickenburg had sold out his interest in 1865, the price supposed to have been $85,000, $20,000 as a down payment. Almost immediately the buyer, B. Phelps of New York, began to haggle with the Austrian saying his title was not clear, partly because of the long lost partners. Believing he could win the case against the big corporation, Henry hired lawyers and sued, spending almost all his $20,000, but the courts held for the company. Broken in spirit, Wickenburg retired to an adobe house by the river.

During the litigation the company had taken out $1,850,000 in gold, built a huge mill at the mine and was erecting many stone buildings as offices, bunk houses, stores and homes for married workers. Adobe structures also sprang up by the dozens until Vulture City was a city in fact.

After a few years of prosperity B. Phelps sold out, having run up against a fault which cut off the main Talmadge vein. The new owners were furious but helpless, having bought the property on the strength of known richness. After many exploratory thrusts they located the continuing vein but then new faults were encountered and the mine

"MILLION DOLLAR STOPE" was so large miners were forced to leave heavy pillars of rich gold-bearing rock as ceiling supports. When later owners began mining out pillars, thousands of tons of rock collapsed into pit, forming huge "glory hole." While some surface ore has been removed since, artificial crater is essentially due to fall of roof.

changed hands again. Subsequent history of the workings followed this pattern until one lucky owner noticed the vein was widening and becoming even richer. The stope got so wide rock pillars were left to support the ceiling composed of many tons of earth and rock. This section was called aptly "The Million Dollar Stope". Then a new owner, a Canadian named McClyde, found himself running short of ready ore to keep the mills going and started mining out the pillars. Before salvage was completed the entire roof fell in, creating a gigantic "glory hole". Many pillars of high assay ore were lost, as was any possibility of locating the direction of the lode.

In 1931 "Rawhide Douglas" put down a shaft near the present well in an effort to relocate the

main body of ore but without success. The present mine owner, Dr. George H. Mangun says: "No one has ever located it. None of our present fancy electro-magnetic and electronics devices has been able to give us any clue. This makes the seventh time the lode has been lost due to faulting in prehistoric times."

During the life of the Vulture mine it has yielded $17 million in gold. Any estimate as to how much this would be increased by persistent "highgrading" could only be a guess, but some old timers say the true total would be near $100 million.

And the discoverer of all this wealth, Henry Wickenburg, lived out his embittered life in the adobe shack down by the river. His health gradually failed and meager savings disappeared. Early in July of 1905 the Austrian, born Heinrich Heintzel, walked out of his home, stopped under a large mesquite tree and blew his brains out. The weapon, an old style revolver, was very likely the same one with which he killed the vulture that showed the way to it all.

LOCALE OF HENRY WICKENBURG'S CAMP the night before he found his gold mine, Vulture Peak in background. Area is veritable botanical garden, displaying large portion of Arizona's 170 known species of cacti. Most conspicuous is huge saguaro, Cereus (properly Carnegea) Gigantea. Unbranched specimen, right of center, is less than 75 years old, at which age branching may begin. In immediate foreground is hoary-appearing "Jumping Cholla", its points readily becoming detached, sticking tenaciously and painfully to any passing object (like this photographer's bare legs.) At Cholla's left is beaver-tail. Long-caned bushes in center are not of cacti tribe, are called ocotillo, every rain bringing to them crop of sparse foliage and terminal racemes of brilliant red blossoms, regardless of season.

19 MEN MET DEATH HERE. During Vulture's early turbulence most murderers and horse thieves came to gruesome end dangling from stout branch of hanging tree. Fights among citizens or workmen resulting in death were condoned but not shooting of residents by strangers. 19th victim of noose was man whose attentions to comely woman were resented by husband who marched culprit to tree at gunpoint. Limb is conveniently low but as one old timer remarked: "We got their feet off the ground." Tree is large specimen of Olneya Tsota, locally called ironwood, general designation for several tough-wooded desert trees.

CONTENTION CITY, ARIZONA

"What is it?" asked the grizzled miner from Tombstone when the waitress in a Contention City cafe set a glass in front of him, informing him it was water. "Oh, that," said the miner. "I've heerd. Even tuk a bath in it onct. Say, miss — will you put it in a bottle or sumpin so I can show it to the boys down home."

Water was scarce enough in Tombstone for ore milling purposes and Contention City was one of the most northerly of the several towns established along a ten-mile stretch of the San Pedro River to process the Tombstone ores and took its name from the big mine owned by partners Ed Schieffelin and Richard Gird. Arizona Pioneer Historical Society records explain the use of the name "Contention":

"Hank Williams was one of the thousands of prospectors who flocked to Tombstone when the word got around that Ed Schieffelin had struck it rich. His camp was close to that of Schieffelin and partner Dick Gird. One of his mules got away and in trailing it he noticed that the animal's halter chains were scraping the dirt off of rich ore. He immediately staked a claim, the location of which was hotly contested by Gird. Williams could not have been very positive about his rights in the dispute; he was persuaded to sell out to Schieffelin and Gird. They developed the claim in question, naming the mine Contention."

As soon as the mill site was established just above the San Pedro on the east bank the town site was bought early in September, 1879 by D. T. Smith and John McDermott. By the middle of the month the partners had surveyed the town, within a week were selling lots and up jumped a hotel, saloon, restaurant, laundry and a hodge podge of shanties. The mill on the bluff, 170 feet long with a depth of 142 feet, was being built and three more expected.

In a year or two the place grew to be a solid city, most buildings of adobe, the available material. By that time there were more businesses with a rash of saloons. The most imposing structure facing the "waterfront" was a railroad station, Contention having achieved the proud distinction of being the railhead for the New Mexico, Arizona and Sonora Railroad. While the line was building, contractors and crews had their headquarters in the town and if there was any danger of Dull Care showing up, the boys kept it safely out in the desert.

When William Henry Bishop visited Contention City in 1882, he wrote of the experience in his book MEXICO AND HER LOST PROVINCES. The section concerning the milling town is reprinted in ARIZONA GUIDE: "We changed horses and lunched at Contention City. One naturally expected a certain amount of belligerency in such a place, but none appeared on the surface during our stay. There were

WHAT BUILDING? While rather extensive, ruins give little or no clue as to nature or purpose of building. Low angle of sunlight brings out surface texture of unfired adobe bricks.

RUINS OF Contention Mining and Milling Co., described as having extended 170 feet along side of rocky cliff. Diligent, thorn-harassed search reveals many remains of wood beams, stamp pistons, rusting tools, cables.

plenty of saloons, the Dew Drop and the Headlight among others, and at the door of one of them a Spanish senorita smoked a cigarette and showed her white teeth.

"Contention City is the seat of the stamp mills for crushing ore which is brought to Tombstone. The latter place is without sufficient water power. The stamps are heavy beams which drop on the mineral on the mortar and pestle plan, with a continuous roar, by night as well as by day. 'That's the music I like to hear', said our driver gathering up his reins. 'There ain't no band ekils it' ".

Today Contention is a silent place except at night when coyotes croon their spine-tingling wails,

sounds very different from that of crashing stamps. An unmarked dirt road approaches a small turning area on the west bank of the San Pedro. Peering from the mesquite brush lining the river banks, the ghost town hunter can sight the remnants of the railroad depot on the other side. One swims the stream, wades or jumps over it, depending on the season, crosses several sand bars — and there is what is left of the town. No building remains intact, the depot only partly preserved. Many adobe ruins are encountered and many mesquite thorns. The mill ruins lay back against the bluff, only foundations and rotting beams remaining.

If the weather is wet the advice is to stay away, this reporter learning the lesson the hard way. It is impossible to get traction on slippery adobe and while wheels are spinning, the sticky stuff piles up on fenders and undercarriage. And several dips in the road fill rapidly with any fall of water.

FRONT ENTRANCE of Contention City's once proud railway depot in horizontal rays of light from low sun frames staghorn cactus and load of fruits.

FAIRBANK, ARIZONA

Fairbank, on the Santa Cruz River and between Contention City and Tombstone, was a supply center for both and way station for drivers hauling ore from mines at Tombstone to the mills at Contention. It was also an important point on the railroad from Guaymas, Mexico and Benson and a stage terminal for mail and express. Generally supposed to be a corruption of "faro bank," the name of the town more likely honors Chicago merchant K. N. Fairbank who had many mining interests in the area. Early Spanish missionaries reported an Indian village named Santa Cruz on the site in 1700. Even today heavy rains will sometimes expose such artifacts as arrowheads and pottery shards.

The river is subject to sudden flash floods, storms on the headwaters in old Mexico will sometimes swell the usually meager flow to a torrent sweeping all before it. One of these floods occurred in September 1890 and the damage was all the more terrifying because it hit in the night when everyone was asleep. The Tombstone EPITAPH reported the flood, the story recounting heroic efforts on the part of a Mr. Salcido owner of a lodging house. He was awakened by the roar of the waters and ran to each room, warning occupants to flee. "He had cleared the rooms and was leaving when the flood struck the front door and filled the house with water before he could get to the back exit to open the door and let the water run through. The water was up to his neck in a moment and he struggled until help arrived and saved him. . . . He was taken to Williams' Drug Store where he recovered from his fright. . ."

But nothing that ever happened in Fairbank was more exciting than the attempt to rob the Wells Fargo car at the turn of the century. Sensational at the time, details seemed to have faded away but were unearthed in a 1912 issue of the long defunct REAL MEN OF ARIZONA. "One affray in which Jeff Milton took part proved not to be scatheless, but resulted in victory for him and the breaking up of a most dangerous gang of train robbers that ever infested the Territory.

"It occurred in February of 1900 in Fairbank. Milton was still in the employ of the Express Co. as a messenger (or guard) on the Mexican run from Benson to Guaymas, and on one of his runs he met Bill Stiles a deputy sheriff of Cochise County. Stiles at that time was joined with Bert Alvord also a deputy sheriff. Both were secretly engaged in depredations of their own, themselves keeping discreetly in the background while they planned hold-

ups without being discovered. The dividing line between law breakers and defenders was a weak and shaky one in those days and participants in the one activity might the next day join the other side, or take both parts on occasion.

"Stiles told Milton he had arranged a good deal in the desert southwest of Tucson and was desirous of having Milton join him in promoting it. Milton replied that this was impossible, as he was on his way to Guaymas. Stiles then asked "you are sure of that, are you? Well, when you start north again be sure and telegraph me so I can meet you in Benson." Milton promised and Stiles went on his way to plan a hold-up of the Wells Fargo train at Fairbank at a time when Milton whose readiness as a gunfighter was legend would not be present.

"As it happened, however, Milton received a telegram from W. F. Owen, the Express Co. Superintendent, ordering him to return north to take the place of a messenger named Jones who had fallen sick. In his hurry to return he failed to notify Stiles, so when the car marked for holdup stopped in the dusk of a winter's day in Fairbank the man whom Stiles least desired to run up against was guarding the treasure.

"Fairbank was a much bigger place in those days and there was a considerable number of packages to hand out. Milton noticed a considerable number of men in the offing, but presumed them to be cowpunchers. As he stooped to pick up another parcel he heard a voice shout out 'Hands up, there, you blankety blank so and sos!' 'What's the matter?' asked Milton. 'Oh, I guess some of the boys are having a little fun,' answered the agent. 'That's mighty poor fun. Somebody is likely to get hurt around here,' responded Milton.

"He had hardly stopped speaking when the 'Hands up' command was repeated by several voices. And the next moment a number of the men opened fire on him with six-guns and Winchester rifles. The gang was comprised of the Owens brothers, Bravo Horn and a certain notorious bad man, murderer, horsethief and all around desperado named Three Fingered Jack Dunlap. 'Damn it, boys, line up, there,' cried a voice above the fusilade. Milton was shot at the start by a ball that shattered his arm just above the wrist. Another ball knocked off his hat and grazed his skull. Tumbling back into the car he jumped for his gun which was ready and loaded and returned to the door. It was so dark, with people running about, some shooting, that it was impossible to know which were friends and which were enemies. Lead pelted the air in all directions, a perfect storm of bullets rained toward him and riddled the car.

"One ball knocked a lump of flesh out of the same arm already wounded. Then still another entered the arm, ranged upward through the bone and shattered an artery. At this juncture he managed to raise his gun and deliver what turned out to be the most effective blow of the whole battle, shooting Three Finger Jack fatally, though the bandit did not immediately die. Milton, fearing he would die or at least faint away, took the key from the treasure safe and tossed it outside into the darkness.

"When the bandits entered the car they took him for a dead man, searched him and the car for the key. They had not provided themselves with dynamite, and having fully counted on capturing the messenger without a struggle they were forced to abandon the robbery. Only a short time had elapsed since the start of the robbery but they had already remained too long. The excited town was already gathering men to battle the gang. Three Fingered Jack was lifted onto his horse, lashed to the saddle and the gang dashed out of town.

"Retarded in their flight by their wounded companion, they heartlessly abandoned him to die. He was found in the brush about nine miles away next day by one of the posses that was scouring the country. He lived long enough to make a confession. A general rounding up of the gang followed. Bill Stiles turned state's evidence, the others were given long terms in the penitentiary. Since then there have been no further attempts to rob a Well Fargo car.

"Milton was given the best attention locally, then hurried to a hospital in San Francisco where surgeons decided they would have to amputate the arm in order to save his life. When this news was transmitted to Milton he protested, 'Now Doc, what good would I be without my arm? If you cut it off the first thing I'll do when I get out is kill the man that did the job, that goes!' The arm was not amputated, Milton lived and regained partial use of it. He later joined the U.S. Immigration Service as a rider along the border."

The ARIZONA GUIDE, published in 1940 credits Fairbank with a population of 50. As of now, no such number is in evidence, though the store still operates in a small way, as does the postoffice. There are a few trailer houses parked back in the mesquite brush. But Fairbank now is a very different place from the roistering stage and train stop it was when Three Fingered Jack, Bill Stiles and their gang attempted to hold up the treasure car there.

THIS STORE, still operating, served Fairbank in early days. Of adobe construction, it has changed little from times when travel consisted of mule trains hauling ore from mines at Tombstone to mills at Contention City.

FRAME BUILDINGS in Fairbank are deserted, sagging, weathered, encroached upon by desert vegetation such as thorny mesquite at right.

CHARLESTON, ARIZONA

It was Red Dog in Alfred Henry Lewis' fiction, historians called it "a place of bloody violence", to Nell Murbarger it was Devil's Den and Muriel Sibell Wolle said: "If the corpse had a gun on him and the fatal shot came from the front, you didn't look for the killer."

All this and much more was Charleston which was connected to Mexico by the San Pedro River and to Tombstone by a constant stream of ore wagons. The ten-mile stretch of the river supplied the water, which Tombstone did not have, to mill the rich gold ore and for like purpose accounted also for the other adobe-built towns along the river — Millville and Contention City.

Perhaps the first white man to build a shelter here was Frederick Brunkow, a German scientist who left his native land under a cloud and wound up in Arizona doing odd jobs. But the School of Mines at Freiburg, Saxony, prepared him for a job

with the Sonora Exploring and Mining Co. and he was valuable in locating several rich silver veins. About 1858 Brunkow found one of his own but his efforts ended with death at the hands of his own peons.

In 1879 Richard Gird and Ed Schieffelin formed the Tombstone Mining and Milling Co. with the help of Gov. Safford. Schieffelin was familiar with the Brunkow location and its advantages as a mill site, having worked for a time in those diggings. Gird agreed with him and a ten-stamp mill was built on the east bank of the San Pedro, water reaching it via a wooden flume from a dam constructed a mile south. Milling activity centered here to be called Millville, the town growing up across the stream known as Charleston.

Strictly a company town, Charleston was solidly constructed of the prevailing adobe material, some buildings with wooden floors and plastered walls.

CHARLESTON is in complete ruin, remnants of once thriving town hard to find. Buildings like these, of stone instead of common adobe have endured in part. Area once supported good stand of pasture grass, now grows drought-enduring scraggly stand of thorny mesquite with spines that often draw blood from too careless ghost town explorer. If and when projected Charleston Dam is completed, San Pedro River's trickle will be converted to vast lake inundating site of Charleston.

MOST IMPOSING RUINS of Charleston-Millville complex are those of Richard Gird's "Big House", standing conspicuously on rise above San Pedro River. Rock foundation may have aided drainage, helping preserve ruins beyond life of others.

Hardly had the town been officially laid out in the winter of 1878-9 when it began its career as head-quarters for bandits, horse thieves, murderers — at least in the public fancy, nourished by many writers of fact and fiction, notably called Red Dog in Alfred Henry Lewis' stories in an Eastern news-paper. Any number of reputable historians refer to Charleston as a place of bloody violence. Alma Ready said the town literally lived and died to the sound of gunfire and quoting Muriel Sibell Wolle in THE BONANZA TRAIL: "No one seemed disturbed when dead men lay in the street. If the corpse had a gun on him and the fatal shot had come from the front you didn't look for the killer. Guns made the law and men had to react in a split second." James G. Wolf who arrived in Charleston in 1883 wrote: "There were four saloons going twenty-four hours a day. All kinds of gambling houses operated con-tinously. There were lots of naughty girls living close to the saloons. . . When paydays occurred at Fort Huachuca many of the soldiers came to Charleston to drink. . . . . ."

Nell Murbarger says in her GHOSTS OF THE ADOBE WALLS: "Here, if we could believe even half

that has been written about the place, was a second Bodie, an embryo Dodge City, a short-lived Devil's Den where dead men littered the streets and gun-smoke drifted over the land like smog."

The other side of the coin is presented by Mrs. Mary Wood who with her husband moved to the town in 1880. The Murbarger book quotes a Tomb-stone EPITAPH interview with her in 1929 when she said: "If you came to Charleston looking for trouble there were plenty of citizens who would have sup-plied you with any amount of it . . . but the honest, law abiding citizen went his way with little if any greater hazards than he faces today in any large city". It may be that Mrs. Wood was unaware of some illicit activities in her community, or as Miss Murbarger suggests, the town came nearer its image of toughness as it grew older. There is one singular fact, according to Mrs. Wood, that while $1,380,336 worth of bullion was shipped out from the mill in one year's time, "not a dollar of it was ever molested by highwaymen."

The two noisy stamp mills ran day and night except when a breakdown occurred, even on Sun-days. Eastern backers of the operation heard about this desecration of the Sabbath and protested to Dick Gird and manager Wood. They were invited to come to Millville and watch the results of a trial layoff over Sunday. They came, and on Sunday they watched with horror as miners indulged in all-day sprees in the town's saloons. And on Monday they watched the bleary-eyed miners stagger back to work, noted the difficulties of reactivating the cooled-down equipment and left town, convinced the men should be busy every day. How many of Charleston's carousers took advantage of one unique feature is not known but Alma Ready in an ARIzona HIGHWAYS article writes of the rare luxury of drinks "on the rocks", the town being the proud possessor of one of the first ice machines in Arizona Territory, even supplying the commodity to Tombstone.

In its busiest period Charleston had four general mercantile stores, meat market, drug store, with two restaurants and two laundries operated by Chinese. Mrs. Hughes' Boarding House, Eagle and Royal Hotels served citizens and transients as did saloons, estimated as five to thirteen. Regular visits to these

drink emporiums by such notables as the McLowery bunch, Clanton gang and Johnny Ringo did not contribute to law and order.

The town had no jail and Constable James Burnett apparently paid himself. Just when a drunk was rowdy enough to arrest is not known but when a public nuisance was collared, Burnett held him at the point of a sawed-off shotgun, tried, convicted and fined him on the spot, pocketing the proceeds.

As for the usual lynchings with stories of twitching bodies dangling from trees and derricks, it seems Charleston only came close to one. A disgruntled employee at the Gird mill, Johnny-Behind-The-Deuce whipped out his gun and shot chief engineer Henry Schneider fatally. Rumblings of a lynching were stymied by removing him to Tombstone and later to Tucson where he broke jail and vanished.

There was a school in Charleston and legend has it that pupils were accustomed to carrying guns like papa did. While supposedly studying the temptation was great to wing a buzzard flying by the window or pin a fly to the wall. But one Professor Wetherspoon had stricter ideas than his prede-

YUCCAS GROW at Pick-Em-Up stage stop, appropriately marked by ancient trunk. Tiny mining community between Tombstone and Charleston was stop only if stage passengers stood beside road to flag down drivers who were instructed to "Pick 'em up".

cessors. He installed a shelf in the cloakroom and ordered all boys to park their six-guns there.

Another tale concerns the largest bordello. School children would wander to the place after school to look in the windows at whatever was going on. When several of the girls announced at home they had decided what to be when they grew up, owners of the house were ordered to move it. The new location was near Fort Huachuca. Christmas came often for the soldiers.

Whether Charleston or neighboring Tombstone should rightly be termed the toughest town in Arizona Territory may be debated for years to come. Contender Charleston offers at least one well-authenticated incident for its side — the murder of young M. R. Peel.

Across the river stood the immense adobe structures of the Tombstone Mining and Milling Co. including offices and residences facing the river, one room containing a safe built of brick. One evening in 1882 the popular company engineer — Peel — was sitting in the office talking with three friends when two masked men threw open the door. Both intruders raised their rifles and fired point blank at Peel, one slug entering his body, the other bury-

ing itself in the adobe wall. Still without a word, the two murderers fled to their horses held by a third man and disappeared in the darkness. Peel's funeral was held in Tombstone with burial in its famous Boot Hill.

The killing seems to be explained only as a boner in a badly planned payroll robbery attempt. One of the gunmen, identified as William Grounds, was shot and killed the following day while "resisting arrest". The other, Zwing Hunt, though wounded, lived to be placed in the Tombstone jail, later recovering and escaping.

Charleston, spawned with Tombstone, died with Tombstone. When Tombstone's already declining mines began filling with water in the '80s, production of ore slowed to a standstill, leaving little excuse for Charleston to linger on. On top of that, the smaller town's once highly profitable underground trade with Mexico was now cut off by the border town of Nogales.

But it was a caprice of nature that wrecked Charleston — a major earthquake occurring May 3, 1887. Thirty minutes of continued shocks reduced the adobe buildings to rubble and the town was never rebuilt. Its birth as a company town had been sudden, its destruction complete in one half hour.

THIS ROOM in Tombstone Mining and Milling Co. buildings housed company safe, constructed of fire brick and closed by substantial iron door. Door has long since vanished but location of safe is shown here, marked by bricks differing from larger unfired adobe ones.

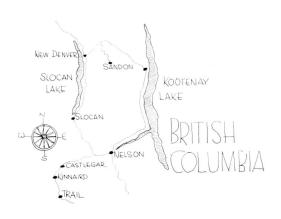

SANDON, BRITISH COLUMBIA

Midnight of May 3, 1900, in the mountain-girt mining town of Sandon, was very quiet. The evening before was one of the gayest in the town's history, a traveling stock company presenting the play *Bitter Atonement* at Spencer's Virginia Hall. The house was filled to capacity and the audience gave the actors a standing ovation when the curtain fell. Then between curtain calls one of the actors dropped a burning cigarette in a waste basket.

At 12:30 fire alarm bells began ringing wildly. Most of the population of the isolated town rushed to the scene of the blaze, attempting to remove belongings and furniture from neighboring, closely packed buildings but it was soon obvious that the town was doomed, with flames leaping from one frame building to the next. Sandon's upstream "suburb" was saved only by the dynamiting of the Canadian Pacific's station which stood at the upper end of the gutted section, the fire not being able to jump the gap. Next morning the entire business section was in ashes. All hotels, theaters, banks and stores had burned away, Victoria's *Daily Chronicle* listing more than fifty buildings destroyed.

All this happened eight years after J. M. "Johnny" Harris discovered silver here, started his fabulous climb to riches and setting a mining boom in action. The mining district once known as the "Silvery Slocans" lies in high, timber-clad country in the fork of the Columbia and Kootenay Rivers, bounded on the east by Kootenay Lake, on the west by parallel Slocan Lake. The whole country is a jumble of mountains, many bearing glaciers, and one of the streams draining into Slocan Lake is the Sandon. A fork of the main stream is Carpen-

ter Creek, the steep hills above it still loaded with silver. The first men to tap this mineral wealth were Jack Seaton and Eli Carpenter who would have reaped great reward had they not quarreled over partnership details and parted in bitterness. Others worked their claims and several more rich deposits in the Silvery Slocans but none developed in spectacular fashion. It fell to J. M. "Johnny" Harris to become the silver magnate of the country.

Johnny spent his early boyhood in the tobacco and cotton fields of Virginia, succumbed to wanderlust at a tender age and wound up in Idaho in 1884. He worked in the gold mines there, still only a boy, then discovered he could sell real estate and opened an office. That lasted until a prospector from the wild country north of Nelson brought him a piece of ore shining with veins of silver. Johnny Harris then knew where his heart's desire lay—in the prospecting tradition—and he headed for the new strike.

He stopped first in Nelson which was in the throes of a mining boom, then moved on up into the really wild country to the north, arriving with a companion at the lower end of Slocan Lake where there was no trail, the shoreline vertical cliffs. The two procured a canoe and started for the outpost camp of New Denver, 35 miles up the lake. Just short of the town, a sudden storm overturned the flimsy craft and they had to swim for it, a day later being lodged in the swankiest flophouse in New Denver. The slighty built Virginian then started hiking up the Sandon River, reached the tributary Carpenter Creek, started digging and almost at once uncovered a fabulous vein of silver. The date was April 7, 1892.

THIS AREA IN SANDON was separated from rest of town for entertainment of single men. Being built on higher ground at lower end it escaped floods that devastated more respectable section. Author drove camper into level area for night to be on hand for morning light, was questioned by town guard then welcomed with apologies. Many relics have been carried off by vandals, thieves.

With the money from the claim Johnny purchased a third interest in an even more promising mine, the Reco. Before the boom was over the area's mines had produced millions and a flourishing town named for Sandon Creek grew up along the canyon. The town was Johnny's baby as was much of the wealth that came out of the ground around it.

At first the silver-lead ore was hauled down a rough, hacked-out trail to New Denver by the crude method of rawhiding—two cowhides wrapped around twin loads balanced on mules and tied to wooden pack saddles. But as Sandon boomed and the silver mines produced tons of rich ore, the need for a railroad became imperative. Two railroads began laying track simultaneously in a race to reach the camp in the mountains. One was a spur of the Great Northern, United States railroad bossed by tough, Canadian-born Jim Hill, the other a branch of the Canadian Pacific, the Kaslo-Slocan Line. The latter, confident of reaching Sandon first, built an elaborate station there in advance. Just as the K-S line drove the last spike beside it, an engine of the competition chugged around the last bend below town. While the K-S bosses and crew celebrated roundly and went to bed, the G N men "accidentally" got a chain around the shiny new station, hooked it to their new engine and dragged it down the tracks a few hundred feet, toppling the proud little edifice into Carpenter Creek. At it turned out, after hostilities were settled and damages paid, there was plenty of ore for both lines to haul and both served the town for several years.

Before the fire Sandon was a city of more than 3,000, a metropolis in the otherwise unpopulated mountains. One of the showplaces was the Reco, built by Johnnny Harris, named for the mine and attracting the elite of the mining world. Another was the Miners' Union Hall, with hardwood dance floor and stage complete with elaborate scenery. There was the Harris Power and Light Building, two newspapers — MINING REVIEW and PAYSTREAK — two banks, two drug stores and Sandon Hospital. This building was in the upper Gulch section and escaped the big fire in 1900 but was consumed by another blaze six years later that took out the Gulch. The town was proud of its ice rink with a hockey team that consistently took first place in British Columbia leagues. The rink had a separate section for curling and there was a ski jump which brought visiting teams from Revelstoke, Nelson and elsewhere. But the fire at the turn of the century wiped out all this.

SANDON WAS BUILT on plank flume enclosing Carpenter Creek shown in foreground. Main street ran over stream, was lined solidly on both sides by many buildings, few remaining after devastating flood of 1955.

The town was originally built on one side of one street; Carpenter Creek, the narrow canyon bottom allowing no more. After the fire Sandon was promptly rebuilt but by confining the stream to a planked flume and covering it with heavy planks, the street had two solid lines of buildings facing it. This double row continued up the broader section of the canyon about a quarter mile, terminating at the narrower Gulch where a more conventional road wound on for several blocks, this too lined solidly with business structures.

The fire was in May, 1900, and in September little eleven-year old Minnie Stewart arrived in Sandon with her mother and stepfather, James Thompson. Born in another famous camp, George-town, Colorado, Minnie did not find her new situation too strange except for the frenzy of rebuilding. The family settled in the Gulch section and Minnie started school in a large tent, since the regular

school house had burned to the ground. Now 76 years old and living in New Denver, Minnie relates the details with some feeling of nostalgia. The school's walls were boards part way up, the rest of canvas, as was the roof. It housed about 30 pupils, Mr. Barron's upper classes and Miss English's lower. In the center was a wood-burner stove enclosed in a sheet metal circulator. A permanent school was soon built on the side hill and the site of the tent school became that of the new M. E. church in a section called Sunnyside. Then came the 1906 fire in the Gulch, burning out almost all the crowded buildings there. When they were rebuilt, water mains were connected to fire hydrants which extended high in the air above deep winter snows.

Not long after Minnie came to Sandon she met Collin Stewart, then 19 and working in the mines. Seven years later they were married and Minnie

CITY HALL was built immediately after great fire of 1900, survived equally destructive flood of 1955, though previously long deserted. As town declined school in higher Sunnyside was abandoned for lack of pupils, reestablished on lower floor of City Hall. It was attended by George Stewart who was born in Sandon and daughter Ivy went to first grade here before family left town. City offices at first filled entire structure, later shriveled to one room on upper floor reached by inside stairway, one shown here used for fire escape. Similar one on another building was first to burn in fire, cutting off escape by tenants.

did not have to change her name. When their first born son George grew older he too worked in the silver mines around Sandon and was married there. His daughter Ivy was born in 1936 and went to school there until 1942 when the entire family group moved to New Denver. Ivy was married there to Perry Anderson of the old mining camp of Ymer, B.C. and the couple has three children. Now the whole line from great-grandmother Minnie Stewart on down lives in one New Denver house. This near ghost town lies on the shore of beautiful Slocan Lake almost in the shadow of a mountain topped by the extensive Lucerne Glacier.

Sandon would likely never have rebuilt after the fire but for the drive of Johnny Harris who could see nothing but a rosy future for his town. The rush to the Klondike had drained away many miners dissatisfied with returns after the silver panic although there was still plenty of the metal left in the Slocans. The city had seen its best days but Harris kept it going even helping finance some slipping mines and there were still some lively events.

One miner's house was built at the edge of Carpenter Creek, just above the flume entrance. His wife tried to talk with her neighbor across the stream, leaned too far out to catch some bit of gossip, lost her balance and fell. She was swept into the flume and down the canyon under the planked street, drowning before reaching the lower open end. And several times sudden melting of snows swelled the stream to proportions that wrecked a building or two and undermined sections of track, leaving rails and ties dangling.

Yet these were minor disasters compared with the news that Johnny Harris was going to make his last home in his native Virginia. Once there in a fine house with luxurious furniture, he wrote Sandon friends he was glad he had returned to his birthplace, that he was enjoying his new life. But in a short time he was back in B.C. "Too many relatives moved in with me," he said.

Sandon was fast fading away but Harris kept up a pretense that the place would one day boom again, and maintained his once plush Reco Hotel to be ready for it. He even retained his electric plant, saying he wanted to have the lights ready when the guests arrived. In September of 1950 he told a Vancouver SUN reporter, Jim Hazelwood: "When big money starts rolling again, Sandon will come to life with a bang." But Hazelwood and his bride, in the town on their honeymoon, were almost the last guests in the old hostelry. Johnny was still full of faith in a comeback for his city when he died there in 1953 at 89.

His death spared him the sight of Sandon's nearly complete destruction two years later. Snows had attained an unusually heavy pack in the winter of 1954-55 and it was slow melting that spring, meeting in June a tremendous electric storm with a deluge of warm rain. A log jam twenty feet high formed in the canyon above Sandon and then broke, releasing a torrent that carried trees, rocks and mud down on the nearly deserted town. The flume was entirely destroyed and almost all buildings carried away or shattered. Johnny's pride, the Reco Hotel, was wrecked, foundations and lower floor carried away, remaining upper floors tipped crazily into the roaring waters. The few remaining inhabitants escaped on foot, crossing the canyon farther down on a railway trestle that was "vibrating and shivering

OLD STRUCTURE in Gulch section above main business section escaped both fire and floods, was office for one of Sandon's physicians, Dr. Gomm. Fire hydrant is barely accessible in summer, more so when snow was deep. Water still trickles from this one.

something awful", according to one of the refugees. The entire canyon was filled with the wreckage of the city and much of the debris remains.

Sandon today is peaceful, though Carpenter Creek still roars down the canyon. The few buildings spared by the flood of June 22, 1955, stand scattered along the stream like the snaggled remnants of an old crone's teeth. In summer half a dozen people live in small houses farther back from the creek in the Gulch, one of them a watchman for remaining mine properties. Visitors are welcome but kept under his scrutiny because of vandalism. The road from Nelson is paved most of the way, becoming narrow but fairly good dirt and gravel near Slocan at the foot of Slocan Lake. The road then follows along the water, often at the very edge, and in one stretch is one-way, squeezed between rock walls and through a rather small tunnel. A sign along the way reads with some understatement: "Pass with caution". There is a five-mile stretch of pavement between Silverton and New Denver, then dirt again and narrower, is strictly one-way in spots to Sandon.

BRICK BUILDING at left was general store known as "Hunter's", at right Virginia Block, built by Johnny Harris from Virginia. Structure contained Harris' offices including those of his water and light works. Both buildings were built in 1900 after fire of that year.

ARRIVAL OF PACK-TRAIN was big event in early day Sandon. Photo by courtesy of British Columbia Provincial Archives.

ROLL CALL OF THE SHADOWS

Publisher's note: The listing makes no pretense of being complete. As this is being written both Mr. Florin and Dr. Mason are in the field photographing and researching the material for additional works to supplement *Western Ghost Towns, Ghost Town Album, Ghost Town Trails, Ghost Town Shadows,* and this book *Ghost Town Treasures,* the fifth in the series.

Towns in large type are treated either in *Western Ghost Towns, Ghost Town Album, Ghost Town Trails, Ghost Town Shadows,* or *Ghost Town Treasures* as indicated. Those in small type are candidates for future publications and are listed for the benefit of the reader who may wish to investigate them himself.

ALASKA

GHOST TOWN SHADOWS—Skagway.

Anvil Creek, Tanana, Niack, Crooked Creek, Eagle, Chicken (Ptarmigan), Jack Wade, Ketchumchuck.

ARIZONA

WESTERN GHOST TOWNS—Chloride, Goldroad, Oatman, Whitehills.

GHOST TOWN ALBUM—Tombstone, Gleason.

GHOST TOWN TRAILS—Mineral Park, Jerome.

GHOST TOWN SHADOWS—McCabe, Bumblebee, Stanton, Congress, Octave, Crown King, Weaver.

GHOST TOWN TREASURES—Ehrenberg, Quartzsite, Salome, Vulture City, Charleston, Contention City, Fairbank, La Paz.

Twin Buttes, Dos Cabesas, Calabasas, Tubac, Mowrey, Washington, Millville, Metcalf, Pierce, Constellation.

BRITISH COLUMBIA

GHOST TOWN TRAILS—Beaver Pass, Richfield, Barkerville, Cameronton, Stanley, Yale, Ashcroft Manor, Copper Mountain, Allenby, Granite Creek, Hedley, Coalmont.

GHOST TOWN SHADOWS—Bennet Lake.

GHOST TOWN TREASURES—Sandon.

Atlin, Waldo, Wardner, Fort Steele, Crow's Nest Landing, Phoenix, Fisherville, Zincton, Wardley, Baynes, Poplar, Silverton, Warnell, Lumberton.

CALIFORNIA

WESTERN GHOST TOWNS—Ballarat, Bodie, Cerro Gordo, Darwin, Masonic, Swansea, Calico.

GHOST TOWN ALBUM—Mariposa, Hornitos, Bear Valley, Sawmill Flats, Columbia, Sonora, Jamestown, Jackson, Vallecito, Murphys, Altaville, Mokelumne Hill, Volcano, Fiddletown.

GHOST TOWN TRAILS—Coloma, Rough and Ready, Sierra City, Downieville, North San Juan, Grass Valley, Nevada City, Timbuctoo.

GHOST TOWN SHADOWS—Weaverville, Douglas City, Whiskeytown, Old Shasta, French Gulch.

GHOST TOWN TREASURES—Gold Camp, Tropico Mine, Randsburg, Garlock.

Hawkinsville, Nortonville, Judsonville, Knob, Sommersville, Empire, Paradise, Panamint City, West Hartley, Happy Camp, Walker, Magnesite Mine.

COLORADO

WESTERN GHOST TOWNS—Animas Forks, Eureka, Gladstone, Kokomo, St. Elmo, Leadville, Silverton.

GHOST TOWN ALBUM—Cripple Creek, Victor, Lake City, Bonanza, Villa Grove, Crestone, Creede.

GHOST TOWN TRAILS — Alma, Breckenridge, Fairplay, Silver Plume, Georgetown, Blackhawk, Central City, Apex, Ward.

GHOST TOWN SHADOWS—Maysville, Shavano, Buena Vista, Poncha Springs.

GHOST TOWN TREASURES—Pitkin, Ohio City, White Pine.

Crested Butte, Gothic, Jack's Cabin, Iola, Tomichi Creek, Crystal, Marble, Romley, Tincup, Telluride, Ashcroft.

IDAHO

WESTERN GHOST TOWNS—Burke, Gem, Idaho City, Murray, Pioneerville, Placerville, Potosi Gulch, Silver City.

GHOST TOWN ALBUM—Leesburg, Shoup, Bayhorse.

GHOST TOWN TREASURES—Warren, Mt. Idaho.

Atlanta, Delamar, Custer, Clayton, Rocky Bar, Triumph, Bitch Creek, Clara.

MONTANA

WESTERN GHOST TOWNS — Bannack, Bearmouth, Beartown, Clancey, Elkhorn, Garnet, Granite, Keystone, Laurin, Mammoth, Marysville, Melrose, Philipsburg, Rimini, Southern Cross, Virginia City, Wickes.

GHOST TOWN ALBUM — Giltedge, Kendall, Maiden.

GHOST TOWN TRAILS—Castle City.

GHOST TOWN SHADOWS—Pony.

GHOST TOWN TREASURES—Landusky, Zortman, Ruby Gulch.

Chester, Yogo Gulch, Gold Creek, Black Pine, Pioneer, Cable, Confederate Gulch, Norris, Greenhorn, Grizzly Gulch, Gold Point, Hecla, Copperopolis, Louisville, Ruby, Emigrant Gulch.

NEVADA

WESTERN GHOST TOWNS — Austin, Belmont, Candelaria, Dayton, Eureka, Fairview, Galena, Goldpoint, Goldfield, Goodsprings, Hamilton, Manhattan, Midas, Tuscarora, Nelson, Pine Grove, Rhyolite, Rochester, Tonopah, Unionville, Virginia City.

GHOST TOWN ALBUM—Washoe, National.

GHOST TOWN TRAILS—Genoa.

GHOST TOWN SHADOWS—Broken Hills, Rawhide, Rockland, Aurora, Ione, Grantsville, Berlin.

GHOST TOWN TREASURES—Paradise Valley.

Shafter, Golconda, Pioche, Osceola, Mountain City, Dinner Station, Jarbridge, Charleston, Jefferson, Rio Tinto, Goldcreek.

NEW MEXICO

GHOST TOWN ALBUM — Tyrone, Magdalena, Kelly, White Oaks, Kingston, Lake Valley, Hillsboro, Pinos Altos.

GHOST TOWN TRAILS—Alma, Mogollon, Elizabethtown.

GHOST TOWN SHADOWS—Shakespeare.

GHOST TOWN TREASURES—Cimarron, Dawson, Koehler, Folsom, Watrous, Brilliant, Gardiner, Colfax.

Folsom, Madrid, Cabezon, Georgetown, Hatch, Chloride, Belen, Golden, San Pedro, Cerillos, Bland, Terrero, Park City, San Marcial, Bonito City, Albemarle, Colmor, Organ.

OREGON

WESTERN GHOST TOWNS — Antelope, Austin, Bonanza, Bourne, Cornucopia, Granite, Grandview, Greenhorn, Hardman, Hoskins, Jacksonville, Kerby, Marysville, Shaniko, Sumpter, Whitney.

GHOST TOWN ALBUM—Auburn, Malheur City, Lonerock, Richmond, Sanger.

GHOST TOWN TRAILS — Paisley, Mabel, Ashwood, Shelburn.

GHOST TOWN SHADOWS—Kings Valley, Chitwood, Kernville, Elk City.

GHOST TOWN TREASURES—Champoeg, Aurora, Butteville, Ortley, Wauna, Buena Vista, New Era, Natal, Mist, Apiary, Goble, Metzger.

Sweden, St. Louis, Paulina, Niagara, Hugo, Galice, Susanville, Wheatland.

SOUTH DAKOTA

GHOST TOWN ALBUM—Cascade Springs, Custer, Hill City.

GHOST TOWN TRAILS — Crook City, Central City, Lead, Terry, Pluma, Preston, Trojan, Deadwood.

GHOST TOWN SHADOWS — Galena, Sheridan, Rochford, Rockerville.

Evarts, Travare, Le Beau, Witten, Carter, Wheeler, Milltown, Tinton, Rockport, Palisade, Dakota City, Haward City, Bon Homme, Fairbank, Parade, La Foon.

UTAH

GHOST TOWN ALBUM—Bingham Canyon, Alta, Mammoth, Park City, Eureka, Silver City.

GHOST TOWN TRAILS—Iosepa, Mercur.

GHOST TOWN SHADOWS—Corinne.

GHOST TOWN TREASURES—Sego.

Standardville, Gold Hill, Fairfield, Silver Reef, Grafton, Spring Canyon, Hiawatha.

WASHINGTON

WESTERN GHOST TOWNS—Blewett Pass, Copper City, Index, Liberty, Skamokawa, Sultan, Trinity, Wilkeson.

GHOST TOWN ALBUM — Northport, Bossburg, Republic, Orient, Curlew.

GHOST TOWN TRAILS — Riverside, Nighthawk, Loomis, Ruby, Conconully.

GHOST TOWN SHADOWS — Port Ludlow, Port Gamble, Home Colony, Union.

GHOST TOWN TREASURES—Maryhill, Frankfort, Knappton, Altoona, Vader, McGowan, Deep River.

Monte Cristo, Roslyn, Ronald, Marble, Garland Springs, Pluvius, Oysterville, Holden, Naselle, Brookfield.

WYOMING

WESTERN GHOST TOWNS—Atlantic City, South Pass City, Diamondville.

GHOST TOWN ALBUM — Encampment Battle Rambler.

GHOST TOWN TRAILS—Medicine Bow.

GHOST TOWN SHADOWS—Opal, Glencoe.

Carbon, Du Noir, Dennison, Gold Hill, Miner's Delight, Viola.

YUKON TERRITORY

GHOST TOWN SHADOWS—Dawson City, Louse Town, Carmacks, Carcross, Closeleigh.

Clear Creek, Forty-Mile, Elsa, Gordon Landing, Dalton Post.

Acknowledgements and Bibliography

My sincere thanks to the many individuals who have helped, librarians, editors and "Old Timers" who once lived in or still maintain residence in some of our old towns.

THE BONANZA TRAIL *by Muriel Sibell Wolle*

PIONEER DAYS IN IDAHO COUNTY *by Sister Alfreda Elsensohn*

DESERT BONANZA *by Marcia Rittenhouse Wynn*

MONTANA PAY DIRT *by Muriel Sibell Wolle*

SHALLOW DIGGIN'S *by Jean Davis*

GHOSTS OF THE ADOBE WALLS *by Nell Murbarger*

STAMPEDE TO TIMBERLINE *by Muriel Sibell Wolle*

GUNNISON COUNTY *by Betty Wallace*

UNIQUE GHOST TOWNS AND MOUNTAIN SPOTS *by Caroline Bancroft*

TROPICO *by Glen A. Settle*

GREAT CALIFORNIA DESERT *by W. Storrs Lee*

GARLOCK MEMORIES *by Paul B. Hubbard*

CIMARRON MEMORIES, New Mexico Magazine *by Hope Gilbert*

DON QUIXOTE OF THE SIX GUNS *by J. Frank Dobie*

THE DAWSON STORY, ELIZABETHTOWN STORY,

    KOEHLER STORY *by Fr. Stanley*

WILLAMETTE LANDINGS *by Howard McKinley Corning*

THE COLUMBIA *by Stewart Holbrook*

PACIFIC GRAVEYARD *by James A. Gibbs Jr.*

NEVADA'S TURBULENT YESTERDAY *by Don Ashbaugh*

THE STORY OF BODIE *by Ella Cain*

OREGON GEOGRAPHIC NAMES *by Lewis A. McArthur*

GHOSTS OF THE GLORY TRAIL *by Nell Murbarger*

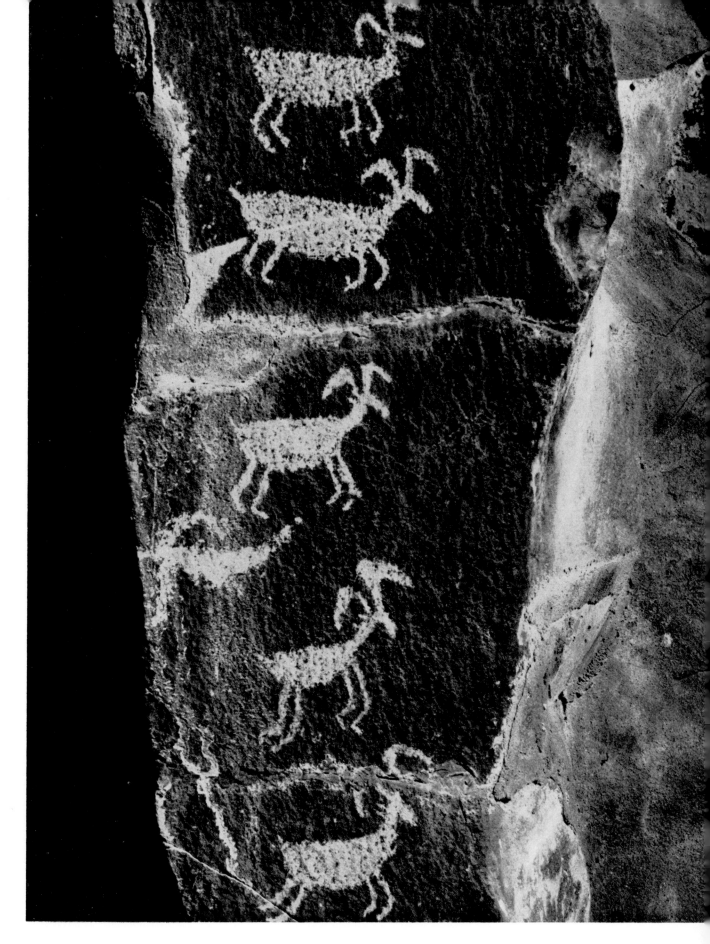